**"Fivefold Operations Volume One: "SHIFTING Into Fivefold Offices & Ministry!"**
This is the first volume of a series of fivefold ministry paradigms written to assist leaders and ministries with understanding fivefold ministry, and SHIFTING into the blueprint of fivefold ministry (e.g. ministry, business, organization). Volume one:

- Provides insights regarding the differences between a traditional church and fivefold ministry and how both are important and needful in the earth.
- Examines the fivefold ministry offices in detail, while exploring their differences from the regular disciple.
- Explores the spiritual gifts and how they differ and flow through believers and fivefold offices.
- Delves into the governmental kingdom positions, how to operate and mature in that seated office of authority, and the importance of licensing and ordination.

Please know you will not only learn these operations, but how to establish them in a fivefold ministry. SHIFT!

Kingdomshifterscec@gmail.com

Kingdomshifters.com

Connect with Taquetta via Facebook or YouTube

All rights reserved. This book is protected by the copyright laws of the United States of America. This book may not be reprinted for commercial gain or profit. The use of occasional page copying for personal or group study is permitted and encouraged. Permission will be granted upon request. Copyright 2019 - Kingdom Shifters Ministries

# Taquetta's Ministry Bio

Dr. Apostle Taquetta Baker is the founder of Kingdom Shifters Ministries (KSM), Kingdom Shifters Empowerment Church, and Kingdom Wellness Counseling and Mentoring Center.

## Credentials

Her expertise to undertake writing instructional books for ministry comes from the following:

- Doctorate in Theological Counseling and Ministry, Rapha Deliverance University
- Master of Science in Community Counseling – Emphasis on Marriage, Children, and Family Counseling, University of Missouri St. Louis
- Bachelor of Science in Psychology, Avila University
- Associate of Arts in Business Administration, Brown Mackie College
- Therapon Belief Therapist Certification, Therapon Institute
- Licensed in liturgical dance, Eagles Dance Institute with Dr. Pamela Hardy
- Ordination as Apostle, Jackie Green Ministries with Dr. Jackie Green
- Board member, New Day Community Ministries, Inc. with Dr. Kathy Williams

Dr. Baker is the author of 31 books and has recorded 2 CD's of prayer decrees.

## Vision

Her expertise is built on many years of faithfully serving her local home church before launching Kingdom Shifters Ministries. At her previous church, she served as a prophet, overseer of the altar workers, and a member of the presbytery. She was used as a member of the Prophetic School team and as the visionary to launch the liturgical dance troupe Shekinah Expressions. She has served on multiple missions' trips to various Caribbean nations and has assisted with planting dance ministries in villages and cities throughout Haiti and Jamaica.

Dr. Baker is on a mission to expand the kingdom of God at every opportunity. She has been gifted in the following areas of expertise for helping likeminded kingdom citizens:

- Empowerment, assistance with launching ministries, businesses, and books;
- Mentoring, counseling, and releasing visions;
- Spiritual warfare, prayer, and administrating apostolic mandates;
- Establishing God's kingdom in individuals, ministries, communities, and regions.

Further, she is passionately committed to training others to understand and embrace destiny.

Please connect to Dr. Baker (Taquetta) through kingdomshifters.com or find her on Facebook.

# TABLE OF CONTENTS

*FIVEFOLD MINISTRY LINGO 1*

*RESPECTING THE TRADITIONAL CHURCH PARADIGM 11*

*FIVEFOLD VERSUS PASTORAL PARADIGM 15*

*OFFICE OF FIVEFOLD MINISTRY 22*

*KINGDOM OFFICER JOURNAL ASSIGNMENT 27*

*ALLEGIANCE OF A KINGDOM OFFICER 31*

*FIVEFOLD OFFICE OPERATIONS 40*

*FIVEFOLD SPIRITUAL GIFTS 87*

*SHIFTING FROM GIFTS TO CALLING 91*

*MATURING INTO THE FIVEFOLD OFFICE 99*

*LICENSING & ORDINATION 103*

# Foreword

The most recent trends in corporate America include who sits at the executive team meeting. In years past, the Human Resources Department was the "hire and fire" arm of the organization. In current models, HR sits at the executive table with talent development and retention strategies. Diversity, organizational change, cultural agility, and strategic leadership are all essential dynamics for any 21st century organization, whether religious or secular. In other words, every successful venture in modern society is based on teamwork. Dr. Taquetta Baker has blended her personal journey, professional expertise, and ministry calling to walk with ministry leaders as they transition from the solo assignment of pastoring to the team paradigm called fivefold ministry. Many times, the suggestion of transitioning gets stuck in the concept of having to lose something or give something up that becomes painful rather than a celebration of embracing fresh ideas. It is much like a basketball team that puts only one player on the floor. That player might be a superstar, but the assignment in its entirety is simply too much for one individual. That superstar player might even win the game, but the wear and tear and overall exhaustion will cause the whole team to pay a price in the bigger picture that was avoidable by utilizing every person. Most of us can easily think of any number of analogies where an individual takes on responsibilities that could be and should be shared with a team. The result of teamwork is increased proficiency and broader influence. That is fivefold ministry in a nutshell.

Dr. Baker has authored this and two successive manuals with steps to activating fivefold ministry. Her model is applicable to ministries of all sizes and arenas, whether a storefront location, neighborhood church, mega church, cell group, business, organization, school, college. Research concerning church attendance shows a drastic reduction in membership and disinterest by many in GenerationX and GenerationY. One of the primary characteristics of Millennials is that they want to be involved and not simply instructed. Traditional church models are set in a hierarchy of disseminating information while fivefold ministry activates spiritual gifts and the individuals who are carrying those gifts. We are in a new season of how people will accept the gospel of

Jesus Christ. We can no longer function in antiquated concepts that are as out of touch with the current time as if we were still pulling out paper roadmaps to chart our route. "Siri, which way to Chicago from my current location?" Fivefold is not about compromising Christianity. It is about exponentially advancing the kingdom vision!

*Dr. Kathy E. Williams*
Founder of New Day Ministries,
Muncie, Indiana

# Foreword

As one that was birthed out of the womb of tradition, denominations and spurning, I found Volume One to be true to my own experience as a recognized fivefold leader, apostle and overseer the past 28 years. As one that is proud to be a Spiritual Mother to Dr. Baker, I prayerfully submit this foreword to launch her even further into her Kingdom writings and teachings. I am amazed and encouraged that this Millennial Gospel Writer will continue produce quality curriculum for future generations that will exalt and edify Jesus Christ and the Kingdom of God.

Each of the three volumes of this work will help the readers "SHIFT" into their destiny and Kingdom positioning. I would label Volume One as the "Appetizer" to fivefold operations. If the reader cannot digest Volume One, the Appetizer, they will not be able to digest the next two volumes. Volume One is a strong Appetizer or Introduction. Volume Two is indeed the Main Course, and Volume Three is the icing on the cake or the Desert.

This is the first of a threefold volume, which is actually an encyclopedia of revelation, foundation and operation of the fivefold ministry offices and giftings in the Lord's Church. Dr. Taquetta Baker is very careful and articulate in choosing her dictionary of terms, painting a picture of a person's destiny process in the Kingdom of God and SHIFTING the reader from milk to meat.

We can all find ourselves in the profound section on moving from traditional church paradigms into the apostolic SHIFT. It is important to distinguish between Christian doctrine, man's doctrine and dogma. So many of our leaders could have been further along in their maturing process but they got stuck in misinterpretation of biblical doctrines. True biblical doctrine is meant to set you free, not bind you. Dogma is man's denominational doctrinal interpretations. But all Holy doctrine is given by the inspiration of the Holy Spirit. This is the doctrine that only comes from God himself.

I love the way Apostle Baker peels away the type of things that cause Believers to reject, leave or stray away from the true fivefold structure that Christ has given us. Most Believers cannot stand true structure, accountability and covenant. The author spends ample time in helping us all deal with our own issues that hinder spiritual growth in the Kingdom of God.

She spends detailed time on each of the fivefold offices as well as bringing clarity on the diversities, differences and cautions when flowing in spiritual gifts in the Church. Yet none of these gifts and offices function well unless they function in love and spiritual maturity.

Finally, I was glad that Dr. Baker addressed the well known statement *"I Do not Need a Title."* The President of the United States never makes a foolish statement like that. For the office itself demands respect and cannot be mistaken for something else. The titles that Christ gave his fivefold officers was never to promote them or cause them to Lord over others. But these titles were given to *"reveal rank and authority over principalities and powers and not for the Body of Christ idolize a person."*

Dr. Baker very clearly states:

> *"When God revealed to me that I was an apostle and I was resistant to embracing the title, he began to show me how some of my warfare was the enemy taking advantage of the fact that I had not become a sign to my ultimate identity in the earth, and that I had not been set in that position. He told me that I needed to position myself to be ordained. The enemy will take your position, your land, your realms, your regions, your authority and your rewards, your blessings, and whatever else you reject or refuse to claim."*

In closing, Volume One book is the strong and truthful Appetizer…"SHIFT"…that the Body of Christ needs to walk fully in the Kingdom authority we have been given. It is a tremendous introduction to the next two volumes and as Dr. Taquetta would say, *"SHIFTING into a fivefold destiny lifestyle."*

*Shifting from Glory to Glory,*
*Bishop Dr. Jackie L. Green - Apostle and Overseer*
*JGM Enternational PrayerLife Institute, Redlands, CA*

# Endorsement

When God ushers us into a new season, He also leads us into the discovery of new truth. This truth is not new to God, but new to us. We need new articulation and revelation to come into higher levels of function and purpose. I call this, *the forerunner anointing*. This manual is written by one of this generation's forerunners, Apostle Taquetta Baker. She skillfully communicates master level revelation to arm you for your assignment.

Forerunners live out ahead and need confirmation of the next level and season. They see into the future and beyond! This is one of the marks of apostolic and prophetic people. They hunger to know the next and are tasked with present truth that will impact future generations. Forerunners must realize that many times they are sowing the seed. This is a Kingdom principle.

I have planted, Apollos watered, but God gave the increase.

> *So then neither is he who plants nor he who waters anything, but God who gives the increase.*
> 1Corinthians 3:6-7

As a forerunner, you may not be the one that sees the full harvest. You may be used by God to plant valuable seed that another will come behind and water. Be okay with that. Be willing to invest in the Kingdom and make a difference. You may be sent to places that are difficult. God appoints the rugged to till the hard ground. It is not a punishment, but a mandate. Apostolic forerunners carry a breaker anointing; to break open the hard ground and SHIFT the territory.

Forerunners must be willing to walk alone at times, carrying the word and the mandate. A forerunner carves a trail for others to navigate. A forerunner discovers the proclamation of the Lord and releases it with no fear.

This manual is not for the casual believer. It is for those who are called to a forerunner mandate to be equipped and charged. Get ready to go to the next level!

*Apostle Ryan LeStrange*
Founder TRIBE/RLM/LeStrange Global LLC & iHubs
Author of Hell's Toxic Trio

# FIVEFOLD MINISTRY LINGO

Some of the information in this chapter comprises of information from Dr. Taquetta Baker's *"Sustaining The Vision Workbook."* This chapter will help the reader get started with clearly understanding and digesting the information in this manual. Continuous study will assist in learning fivefold ministry lingo that will be essential for cultivating an efficient fivefold ministry paradigm, lifestyle, and ministry culture.

<u>Nature</u> is the reality of who we are. It is the bottom line foundation of who we are. Nature is the essence of who we are. Our nature is the origin, constitution (laws and principles), and inherited character of who we are. The nature of who we are cannot be changed.

<u>Character</u> is the collection of features and traits that forms the nature of some person or thing. Character encompasses the qualities, uniqueness, peculiarities, personality traits, behaviors of a person or thing. The essence of our true godly character is always innate within us. This is the reason an evil person can perform a good act or be loving one minute and evil the next. Our character, however, can be influenced where our personality begins to manifests qualities, behaviors, etc., that is contrary to our true godly character. But the essence of character is still there. It is dormant as our personality operates

<u>Identity</u> The world would say that identity was being one's authentic self. I define healthy identity as being who God created us to be. Biblically, identity means being created in the likeness and image of God as *identity* began in the garden with Adam and Eve.

> *Genesis 1:26* And God said, Let us make man in our image, after our likeness: and let them have dominion over the fish of the sea, and over the fowl of the air, and over the cattle, and overall the earth, and over every creeping thing that creepeth upon the earth.

> *The Message Bible* God spoke: "Let us make human beings in our image, make them reflecting our nature So they can be responsible for the fish in the sea, the birds in the air, the cattle, And, yes, Earth itself, and every animal that moves on the face of Earth."

<u>*Image* is *selem* in Hebrew and means:</u>
1. to shade; a phantom, i.e. (figuratively) illusion
2. resemblance; hence, a representative figure, especially an idol
3. image, vain shew

<u>*Likeness* in Hebrew is *dmut* and means:</u>
1. resemblance; concretely, model, shape; adverbially, like
2. fashion, like (-ness, as), manner, similitude

Dictionary.com defines of *likeness* as:
1. a representation, picture, or image, especially a portrait
2. the state or fact of being like
3. the semblance or appearance of something; guise
4. correspondence in appearance; something that corresponds
5. Synonyms: affinity, agreement, alikeness, analogousness, analogy, appearance, carbon, clone, comparableness, comparison, conformity, copy, counterpart, dead ringer, delineation, depiction, ditto, double, effigy, equality, equivalence, facsimile, form, guise, identicalness, identity, image, knock-off, lookalike, model, parallelism, photocopy, photograph, picture, portrait, replica, representation, reproduction, resemblance, sameness, semblance, similarity, simile, similitude, study, uniformity, Xerox

Dictionary.com defines *identity* as:
- the state or fact of remaining the same one or ones, as under varying aspects or conditions
- the condition of being oneself or itself, and not another
- condition or character as to who a person or what a thing is
- the state or fact of being the same one as described
- the sense of self, providing sameness and continuity in personality over time and sometimes disturbed in mental illnesses, as schizophrenia
- exact likeness in nature or qualities
- an instance or point of sameness or likeness

A healthy identity is birthed through relationship with God. We have a healthy identity when we understand:

- ✓ Who God is and is not (our creator and ruler)
- ✓ Who we are and are not (our identity and purpose)
- ✓ That we are a unique Xerox copy of God and are made in his image, therefore we have his capabilities and authorities in us
- ✓ Can actively live in our authentic self, based on who God is and who we are through God (our destiny and generational inheritance through him)

**Blueprint** is God's specific design for how we are to journey in destiny and produce his vision in the earth. When not implemented as he desires, can cause an altering of destiny and the vision and even death. Many people equate their success to the progress they are making and the fruit their destiny and vision is producing. God equates success by obedience and whether we are producing his designed will in the earth.

**Calling** is what we are anointed or appointed to do.

**Destiny** is where we are going in life. Destiny is a progressive journey with God. We all have destiny moments of success, but destiny is a lifestyle journey with the Lord.

> *Genesis 1:26-28 And God said, Let us make man in our image, after our likeness: and let them have dominion over the fish of the sea, and over the fowl of the air, and over the cattle, and over all the earth, and over every creeping thing that creepeth upon the earth. So God created man in his own image, in the image of God created he him; male and female created he them. And God blessed them, and God said unto them, Be fruitful, and multiply, and replenish the earth, and subdue it: and have dominion over the fish of the sea, and over the fowl of the air, and over every living thing that moveth upon the earth.*
>
> *Proverbs 19:21 Many plans are in a man's mind, but it is the Lord's purpose for him that will stand.*
>
> *Psalm 119:105 Your word is a lamp to my feet, and a light to my path.*
>
> *Psalms 139:13-17 For thou hast possessed my reins: thou hast covered me in my mother's womb. I will praise thee; for I am fearfully and wonderfully made: marvellous are thy works; and that my soul knoweth right well. My substance was not hid from thee, when I was made in secret, and curiously wrought in the lowest parts of the earth. Thine eyes did see my substance, yet being unperfect; and in thy book all my members were written, which in continuance were fashioned, when as yet there was none of them. How precious also are thy thoughts unto me, O God! How great is the sum of them!*
>
> *Jeremiah 29:11 - For I know the thoughts that I think toward you, saith the LORD, thoughts of peace, and not of evil, to give you an expected end.*
>
> *Jeremiah 1:5 - Before I formed thee in the belly I knew thee; and before thou camest forth out of the womb I sanctified thee, [and] I ordained thee a prophet unto the nations.*

**Vision** is the journey and plans our lives will take to operate in our calling and achieve destiny.

> *Habakkuk 2:1-4 I will stand upon my watch, and set me upon the tower, and will watch to see what he will say unto me, and what I shall answer when I am reproved. And the Lord answered me, and said, Write the vision, and make it plain upon tables, that he may run that readeth it.*
>
> *For the vision is yet for an appointed time, but at the end it shall speak, and not lie: though it tarry, wait for it; because it will surely come, it will not tarry. Behold, his soul which is lifted up is not upright in him: but the just shall live by his faith.*

**Founder** is a person or group of people who starts, and establishes a ministry, business, organization. They provide the basis, ground work, or blueprint for something that is being established.

**Pioneer** – a person who is first to enter or settle in a region, occupation, sphere of influence. It is a person who is first to do a work in a specific area of influence.

**Trailblazer** – a person who blazes or pioneer a trail for a specific work, occupation, region, or sphere of influence, that others can eventually utilized. They are forerunners sent in advance to create, anoint, establish, and cultivate a work or pathway for others.

**Vision Carrier** is a person God has required to use to birth and/or advance a vision in the earth. Vision carriers embodied the spiritual and natural ability to carry, birth, plant, plow, build, and establish God's plan and purpose in the earth; whether that be via ministry, business, organization, school, college, center, club, book, etc. This vision is instilled at birth. God gives clear instructions to the vision carrier for how to bring the vision to pass.

> *Romans 8:29-31 For whom he did foreknow, he also did predestinate to be conformed to the image of his Son, that he might be the firstborn among many brethren. Moreover whom he did predestinate, them he also called: and whom he called, them he also justified: and whom he justified, them he also glorified. What shall we then say to these things? If God be for us, who can be against us?*

**Talents** are skills and abilities that we do well. All talents are not listed in the bible but are a grace, uniqueness, and ability to do something with supernatural uniqueness and ability that others may or may not have, and even if they do have it, it is not a prototype of you or your talent. An example of talents would be playing the piano, a musical instrument, singing, being a great athlete, being a genius, skilled at math, etc. If you do it well and it comes naturally to you, it is probably a talent that God supernaturally gifted you with.

Talents can also be skills and abilities learned out of need that we do well because of the destiny, calling, or spirit of excellence that is upon our lives. These talents can be utilized to fill a position or need but are not our destiny or calling. It is essential to relinquish these positions and duties as others join the team or ministry and have a destiny and calling in these areas.

**Gifts** are spiritually empowered in us through God's Holy Spirit. They are gifts that God has given for the purposes of saving the lost, bringing deliverance and healing to people, lands, and regions, and establishing God's kingdom in the earth.

## Spiritual Gifts in the bible:

| • **Romans 12:6-8** | • **1 Corinthians 12:8-10** | • **1 Corinthians 12:28** |
|---|---|---|
| • Prophecy<br>• Serving<br>• Teaching<br>• Exhortation<br>• Giving<br>• Leadership<br>• Mercy | • Word of wisdom<br>• Word of knowledge<br>• Faith<br>• Gifts of healings<br>• Miracles<br>• Prophecy<br>• Distinguishing between spirits<br>• Tongues<br>• Interpretation of tongues | • Apostle<br>• Prophet<br>• Teacher<br>• Miracles<br>• Kinds of healings<br>• Helps<br>• Administration<br>• Tongues |

**Anointing** means to smear or rub with oil or perfume for either private or religious purposes. Anointing is a literal oil used to anoint people, places, and things for the purposes of prayer and consecration. Anointing is also wells to which our gifts flow through. These wells help to determine how we operate in our calling. For example, I am called to be an apostle but flow through the anointing wells of warfare, deliverance, and healing. As we seek to define and distinguish our calling, knowing our anointing wells is essential to understanding how the presence of God operates through our lives.

*Isaiah 61:1* *The Spirit of the Lord GOD is upon me, Because the LORD has anointed me To bring good news to the afflicted; He has sent me to bind up the brokenhearted, To proclaim liberty to captives And freedom to prisoners.*

*James 5:14* *Is anyone among you sick? Then he must call for the elders of the church and they are to pray over him, anointing him with oil in the name of the Lord.*

## Fivefold Governmental Offices

*Ephesians 4:11-13*

1. Apostles
2. Prophets
3. Evangelist
4. Pastor
5. Teacher

**Sevenfold Spirit Of The Lord** In addition to being born with talents and gifts, born in gifted offices, and pursuing supernatural gifts, the Spirit of the Lord can rest upon you with an anointing and qualification to judge through the intellect and mind of God.

*Isaiah 11:2* *And the spirit of the Lord shall rest upon him, the spirit of wisdom and understanding, the spirit of counsel and might, the spirit of knowledge and of the fear of the Lord. And shall make him of quick understanding in the fear of the Lord: and he shall not judge after the sight of his eyes, neither reprove after the hearing of his ears: But with righteousness shall he judge the poor, and reprove with equity for the meek of the earth: and he shall smite the earth: with the rod of his mouth, and with the breath of his lips shall he slay the wicked.*

## Gifts Make Room

*Proverbs 18:12* *says, "A man's gift maketh room for him, and bringeth him before great men."*

We tend to equate this scripture to our capabilities and talents. However, the word *gift* in this scripture means, "*offerings, presents, reward, gift.*" It is really when we are giving our gifts as a blessing to others that makes room for us and SHIFTS us into greatness. This is essential to recognizing that our gifts and talents have purpose. They are to empower someone's life, the earth, and the world at large. We must pursue God for how he desires us to impact others, the earth, and the world, so we can be the greatest person he desired us to be. SHIFT!

**Strategy** is a buzz word we tend to hear in this day and age where we have come to recognize that as God speaks, we also need strategy to implement what he is saying. This is good because God's words tend to be progressive and requires movement and work along with faith to manifest them.

**Remnant** entails the group of people we are called to impact.

**Metron** is the sphere of influence and authority a person is called to as it relates to one's gifts and callings. Operating outside of one's metron can cause unnecessary warfare and challenges.

> ***2Corinthians 10:13-16 The Amplified Bible*** *We, on the other hand, will not boast beyond our legitimate province and proper limit, but will keep within the limits [of our commission which] God has allotted us as our measuring line and which reaches and includes even you.*
>
> *For we are not overstepping the limits of our province and stretching beyond our ability to reach, as though we reached not (had no legitimate mission) to you, for we were [the very first] to come even as far as to you with the good news (the Gospel) of Christ. We do not boast therefore, beyond our proper limit, over other men's labors, but we have the hope and confident expectation that as your faith continues to grow, our field among you may be greatly enlarged, still within the limits of our commission, So that [we may even] preach the Gospel in lands [lying] beyond you, without making a boast of work already done in another [man's] sphere of activity [before we came on the scene].*
>
> ***Romans 12:3*** *For I say, through the grace given unto me, to every man that is among you, not to think of himself more highly than he ought to think; but to think soberly, according as God hath dealt to every man the measure of faith.*

*Measure* in Greek is *Metron* and means: *"a determined quantity, extent, portion measured off, measure or limit' or, in other words, a sphere of authority, anointing and influence."*

When we know our metron, we are more effective with operating in our destiny and calling and in advancing the gospel of Jesus Christ. The power and authority we possess without our destiny and calling becomes evident and tangible, and signs follow our kingdom workings.

**Region** is an area of interest, activity, pursuit, etc., a field, community, city, state, nation, or sphere of influence that God has called one to live in, release a vision in, or minister in. It is important to be obedient to releasing the vision when and where God says and to seek him for the reason he has chosen a particular sphere of influence. It is also important to release the vision where God desires because God has instilled specific thoughts, revelation, and decrees into your region, and as you awaken what God has invested in the region regarding you, the region will begin to work with you to produce your destiny and vision in the earth.

> *Isaiah 49:1-4 Listen, O isles, unto me; and hearken, ye people, from afar; The Lord hath called me from the womb; from the bowels of my mother hath he made mention of my name. And he hath made my mouth like a sharp sword; in the shadow of his hand hath he hid me, and made me a polished shaft; in his quiver hath he hid me; And said unto me, Thou art my servant, O Israel, in whom I will be glorified. Then I said, I have laboured in vain, I have spent my strength for nought, and in vain: yet surely my judgment is with the Lord, and my work with my God.*
>
> *New Living Bible Listen to me, all you in distant lands! Pay attention, you who are far away! The Lord called me before my birth; from within the womb he called me by name. He made my words of judgment as sharp as a sword. He has hidden me in the shadow of his hand. I am like a sharp arrow in his quiver. He said to me, "You are my servant, Israel, and you will bring me glory." I replied, "But my work seems so useless! I have spent my strength for nothing and to no purpose. Yet I leave it all in the Lord's hand; I will trust God for my reward."*

**Revival** consists of restoring our lives, families, and regions to the original state God intended us to live before the fall of man in the Garden of Eden, and after Jesus came to redeem us to eternal life. Revival is not fleeting, seasonal, a program or series of services intended to evoke the presence of God. Revival is an eternal part of our right as believers as it was always God's desire for man to be blessed and to prosper and live a daily lifestyle of rejuvenated destiny.

> ***Genesis 1:28*** *And God blessed them, and God said unto them, Be fruitful, and multiply, and replenish the earth, and subdue it: and have dominion over the fish of the sea, and over the fowl of the air, and over every living thing that moveth upon the earth.*

**Revival Reformation** is the concept to establish kingdom reform by infiltrating region with businesses, stores, schools, entertainment, social service agencies, political mandates, and mindsets, etc. This reformation is essential to the world being drawn to God and his kingdom rather than the saints relying on the world's kingdom to cultivate their life and destiny. This is also essential for the region SHIFTING into the likeness of God's kingdom, where his governmental rule is evident and eternal. Revival reformation is implemented by training, equipping and releasing people into their destiny and life's vision for the purposes of infiltration, overtaking, and displacing demonic and worldly systems with the kingdom of God.

**Culture** is the cultivation of an environment with particular beliefs, standards, orders, and behaviors that assists in revealing the character and nature of God and his kingdom.

**Climate** is the cultivation of prevailing attitudes, standards, or environmental conditions that create an atmosphere for God and his kingdom.

**Doctrine** is a particular principle, position, system, or policy taught or advocated, as of a religion or government to instill order to people, a ministry, or organization.

**Paradigm** is a model, doctrine, constitution, or framework containing the basic assumptions, ways of thinking, patterns, and methodologies used to define a people, group, or organization.

**Demonic Systems** consists of principalities, territorial spirits, powers, rulers of darkness, spiritual wickedness in high places.

> ***Ephesians 6:12*** *For we wrestle not against flesh and blood, but against principalities, against powers, against the rulers of the darkness of this world, against spiritual wickedness in high places.*

As saints, fivefold ministers, and ministries, we are to be contending against these demonic systems by demolishing and displacing darkness and wickedness. We should be gatekeeping lands, regions, and spheres while contending against witchcraft, satanism, idolatry, demonic high places and covens, demonic cultures and trends, demonic ideologies, laws, and falsehoods, demonic religious counterfeits, and hell itself.

**World Systems** One may have heard charismatic ministers speak of the seven mountains. These mountains speak of the world systems that many believe we are to infiltrate and overtake. They are as followed:

1. Government
2. Media
3. Arts and entertainment
4. Business
5. Education
6. Religion
7. Family and generations

Though infiltrating and attempting to overtake these mountains is beneficial, I believe we are to establish our own mountains and draws souls and influences away from the world's systems to God's kingdom. The world system is full of policies laws that are contrary to standards of God. They are full of perversion, idolatry, pride, and self-exaltation of which laws are created to justify their freedom to live godlessly. We definitely need more Christian lawmakers. We do not have enough kingdom influence within the government arena to SHIFT laws to godly standards where we can make a sufficient impact in all the other world systems. We do have a right to freedom of speech and to serve our God – the Lord and Savior Jesus Christ, so as we create our own ministry, businesses, organizations, entertainments, platforms, etc., we can implement godly standards where those who come an partake of our mountains have to respect and abide by.

# RESPECTING THE TRADITIONAL CHURCH PARADIGM

As the church age SHIFTS into fivefold ministry and nontraditional blueprints, more and more hate, criticism, and murder are spewed towards the traditional church. Many people who feel like they have "arrived" by SHIFTING out of the traditional and religious system go on a life's mission to "expose" and "shut down" the traditional church. This can be easy to do, especially if one has experienced frustration, church hurt, or have recognized the potential of fivefold ministry and strived to implement it in the traditional church but was rejected. Also, many people become challenged by the religious orders regarding the doctrines of traditional church. Doctrines are manmade, yet we blame God and the constructional church methodology itself for the challenges within them. But doctrines are man's way to set order and structure. Please understand that even in fivefold ministry, though it possesses greater liberties, there will always be structure, order, biblical standards, and a foundation of holiness and Godly character for every blueprint.

*There will always be structure, order, biblical standards, and a foundation of holiness and Godly character for every blueprint.*

With this understanding, we must recognize that some traditional churches are thriving in the vision they have established and are productive in saving souls, discipling people, impacting lives, families and communities, and being effective pillars in the earth. We need to respect this truth and know that each of our blueprints are valuable in advancing the kingdom of God in the earth. Though ideal, everyone is not going to SHIFT to a fivefold ministry paradigm, and that is okay.

Some people are thriving in traditional churches. Some of them are actually aligned with destiny and are working the plan of God for their lives. We cannot assume that all traditional churches are unfruitful and now that we have revelation of fivefold, all who are not like us should be castrated.

When we castrate others, who are doing a different work, we become a kingdom that is divided unnecessarily. We all matter. And if we are honest, most of us started out in and truly needed a traditional church at one time. Even Jesus said if they have and add value to us.

> ***Luke 9:49-50*** *And John answered and said, Master, we saw one casting out devils in thy name; and we forbad him, because he followeth not with us. And Jesus said unto him, Forbid him not: for he that is not against us is for us.*

> ***Mark 9:38-39*** *And John answered him, saying, Master, we saw one casting out devils in thy name, and he followeth not us: and we forbad him, because he followeth not us. But Jesus said, Forbid him not: for there is no man which shall do a miracle in my name, that can lightly speak evil of me. For he that is not against us is on our part. For whosoever shall give you a cup of water to drink in my name, because ye belong to Christ, verily I say unto you, he shall not lose his reward.*

One's mandate is never to kill others who advance the kingdom. People are lying on Jesus if you think he called them to this.

One of the greatest revelations God revealed to me during a frustrating time in ministry where a traditional pastoral paradigm was occurring though the perception and the potential of the ministry was a fivefold paradigm, was that the paradigm vision itself was producing exactly what it was supposed to be producing. God showed me that I could not be aggravated by potential as potential is not reality. I could not be mad at them speaking potential, preaching potential, prophesying potential. This was him revealing revelation of capability, but it still was not reality if it was not implemented as physical vision. If I wanted to live in reality of fivefold, I needed to go to a true fivefold ministry or build a true fivefold ministry. I was operating in false expectations and potential. Potential is nothing more than fantasy or imagery that has not been actualized. One cannot build upon fantasy and imagination and think they are going to produce tangible results. This is not even faith as faith has substance.

> ***Hebrews 11:1*** *Now faith is the substance of things hoped for, the evidence of things not seen.*

The word actually tells us to cast down vain potential aka imagination.

> ***2Corinthians 10:5*** *Casting down imaginations, and every high thing that exalteth itself against the knowledge of God, and bringing into captivity every thought to the obedience of Christ.*

Potential is vain when it is not exercised. And one cannot make a leader exercise a vision that they themselves do not have vision for, time for, room for, desire for, mandate for, manpower for or the ability and confidence to train and equip, so that one can bring it forth. One cannot make a leader be something to them from a fantasy world of their potential that is not the reality of the truth they are living. Sighhhhhh!

As an apostle who has had to BUILD IT, and has only cultivated a fivefold ministry, I need to let it be known that some people need the traditional pastoral type churches! Some people cannot thrive in fivefold ministry.

I have had people come to my ministry and leave because:

- They need the structure. Some people need the traditional and religious rules, regulations, orders.
- Some of us needed them for a season then we grew in our relationship and walk with the Lord where we could sustain without them. Some people cannot live without this type of structure and find it difficult operating through a nontraditional blueprint.
- Some people cannot sustain without the traditional Sunday services and faithful preached word.
- They need this to help them hear from God or in order to know how to embrace him from week to week.
- They cannot hide in the pews. They just want to chill, receive God in their own comfortable way, be encouraged, and receive.
- They do not want the responsibility of building their destiny and life's calling.
- They want the life they have chosen rather than the life God has ordained for them.
- They do not want all the responsibility that comes with discipleship, destiny, and true fivefold ministry.
- They do not want true accountability, covenant, and folks in their business as true fivefold seeks personal relationship with every member in order reveal, train, equip, and release people in their destiny and calling. Also, the concept of covenant in fivefold requires a level of closeness and vulnerability that is not always available in a traditional church.
- They do not want to build from scratch.
- They do not want to build through the strategic blueprint of God as this is time-consuming, can take years, and it entails too much self-sacrificing.

- ❖ They want their children's church where they can get a break and chill with Jesus.
- ❖ They want children's church where someone else is teaching their children about God and how to behave in church and in the world.
- ❖ They need an already ready-made church with all the comfortable fixings.
- ❖ They want to choose which part of the Bible they want to listen too.
- ❖ Some people are used to the traditional church and are comfortable with it.

## *Homework Explorations:*

1. Spend time repenting for any bashing you have done against the traditional church. Spend time blessing them and thanking God for ways you have been blessed by them.
2. Ask God to give you a heart and regard to bless all ministries that are truly of him, even if they are not like you. Spend time in prayer until this is fully birthed and established in you.
3. Ask God to help you to discern and respect those who will come to your ministry but then leave because they would glean better from a traditional setting. As this would occur, bless them rather than curse them. Remain in fellowship as a way of unifying the body of Christ.
4. Ask God what in your character need to mature so you can deem all ministries that are of him valuable. Do what he says to mature in these areas.

# FIVEFOLD VERSUS PASTORAL PARADIGM

Often leaders and/or ministries claim to be operating in fivefold ministry but are truly flowing in a pastoral paradigm. A pastoral paradigm is a traditional church methodology where the pastor is the main minister, leader, decision-maker, and everything regarding the ministry operates through his/or mantle. A fivefold ministry paradigm is founded upon *Ephesians 4* where the roles of Apostle, Prophet, Evangelist, Pastor, and Teacher establishes Jesus' biblical blueprint of team ministry, utilized to disciple, train, equip, empower, release, and cover people as they grow in their walk with God, destiny, and life visions that advance God's kingdom.

> *Ephesians 4:11-12 states The Amplified Bible And His gifts were varied; He Himself appointed and gave men to us, some to be apostles (special messengers), some prophets (inspired preachers and expounders), some evangelists (preachers of the Gospel, traveling missionaries), some pastors (shepherds of His flock) and teachers. His intention was the perfecting and the full equipping of the saints (His consecrated people) that they should do the work of ministering toward building up Christ's body (the church).*

This is confusing and conflicting to people who hear "fivefold" and think they are about to experience team ministry and be disciples trained, equipped, empowered, and released in their destiny and calling. When quite the opposite happens, along with being constantly corrected and "put in one's place," told one is prideful, are seeking validation, and usurping authority as continuous seeking training, equipping, and release confounds matters. Especially if this is not the person's heart or focus, and they are simply seeking the fivefold ministry vision that is being eluded but is not the reality of the ministry at hand. Many leaders and ministries who desire to SHIFT into true fivefold ministry need educational training and mostly likely deliverance from the pastoral paradigm and do not even realize it.

As one would examine my construct of pastoral versus the fivefold paradigm, please note that my heart is not to offend or dishonor pastors or traditional ministries. As one who has launched a ministry, I know all too well the sacrifices that incur from leading a ministry. I also will admit that if I had to operate through a pastoral paradigm, I would not be very successful. I want to take a moment to praise all the pastors who have helped to advance the body of Christ. I appreciate you, and I know God does too. THANK YOU!

**Characteristics Of A Pastoral Paradigm**

- The leader is the head of the ministry.
- The leader does most of the teaching, preaching, services, counseling, overseeing meetings, caring, covering, assisting, shepherding of the sheep, and may only allow others to assist when his/her absence cannot be avoided.
- The leader focuses more on nurturing and caring for the members, particularly of their soul and body.

> *The leader focuses more on nurturing and caring for the members, particularly of their soul and body.*

- Because of the workload, leaders often sacrifice their marriage, relationships with children, family time, vacations, for the sake of the ministry. Burnout and pressure are more prevalent and can be accepted as part of the paradigm and pastoral calling.
- Members partake of the messages and teachings while seeking to implement them in their daily lives.
- Most messages focus on evangelism, salvation, encouragement, soul and body healing, and helping people to survive everyday challenges. There are some dynamic pastoral leaders who can uniquely minister a word that transforms lives and set the captives free.
- Most services occur on Sundays; a weekday service, prayer meeting, Sunday school, and/or bible study may also occur. Though the leader strongly encourages attendance, many members tend to fit services into their schedule rather than see them as an essential part of their lifestyle. The cares of life can sometimes override attending services. There are also some members who faithfully attend services on Sunday and throughout the week, and believe their lives cannot thrive without them.

- Ministries are traditionally housed in church buildings. Some ministries began and are housed in small groups meetings, home churches, storefronts, then move to traditional church settings.
- Though not always the case and not generally the focus, the greater works of deliverance, healings, miracles, signs, wonders, living and operating through the supernatural is minimal.
- The pastoral paradigm is rooted in a doctrine (Baptism, Pentecostal, Protestant, Nondenominational, Methodist, etc.). Doctrine drives the foundational vision, principles, standards, and order of the ministry.
- The doctrines are often religious and traditional in nature, and though many of the standards are essential for godly living, depending on the leader and how the doctrine is utilized, some doctrines may limit the liberty of the Holy Spirit, and the movement and momentum of effectively advancing the kingdom. I also want to note that some religious and traditional ministries are full of the Holy Spirit, flowing of the gifts even though doctrinally rooted. The leader, cultivation of the atmosphere, fellowship one to another, and the heart and purity of the people draws and harness the presence of God.
- Due to the responsibilities of the pastoral leader, doctrinal constitution, focuses of the messages, programs, and services, the pastoral paradigm can sometimes be limited in being able to SHIFT people into living in the fullness of Christ. Leaders may also be too extended to fulfill all that is required to SHIFT people into the fullness of Christ.
- Many pastoral paradigms have a board who enforce the doctrinal vision and may even be able to override the main leader through voting procedures. Many leaders may not be able to advance beyond pastoral paradigms even if they wanted to because of the constitutions set and implemented by the ministry board.
- The leader may have a few assistants and department heads that support and operate through the pastoral paradigm. These leaders are usually unable to implement their own ideologies, suggestions, visions, without the leader's permission. Especially if they sway from the foundational doctrinal vision or the direction the leader is taking the ministry in at that time.
- Members work various positions within the ministry to assist with it working successfully. Often these positions are rooted in gifts, talents, personal enjoyment/desires, or necessity rather than the person's destiny and calling. Many tend to stumble into their destiny and calling while laboring in various areas within the ministry.

- In many pastoral paradigms, there may be emphasis on walking in one's destiny and calling, but minimal opportunities to be utilized, trained, equipped, and released within a pastoral paradigm. If opportunities are available, they are often rooted in the ministries' doctrine and belong to the ministry, rather than the person who pioneered them. Often people feel obligated to remain in pastoral paradigms because they have released their visions within these sects, and cannot take them with them when they desire to leave or advance beyond the pastoral vision. I do not think this is due to maliciousness but simply a lack of education as we often assume that what we do within a ministry belongs to God and that ministry. As one who has helped others launch their destinies and life's visions, I learned through happenstance that as I assist people in these areas, their ministries and businesses are an extension of my ministry and the body of Christ. They were birthed from their loins and thus belonged to them and go with them as they advance with God.
- Because of the limited opportunities general pulpit messages and teachings rather than consistent hands-on mentoring in one's destiny and calling, some members are not built up where they can sustain without the leader and the ministry setting. Minimal members are built up to flourish in their calling, and often positions are given based on favor, faithfulness, and loyalty with the leader than God-ordained or destiny driven.
- In most cases, the ministry is financially supported by tithes and offerings. Some leaders and their department heads may receive financial support if they work full-time positions and if the ministry can afford it. Rarely is there any other stream of income, and most leaders work a secular job or have to create their own stream of income to survive because of insufficient salaries from the ministry.
- Much of the ministries' services, salvation, evangelism, community programs is done within the four walls of the church. There is minimal focus on community impact and regional revival reformation.
- Many community services are limited and are usually based on volunteer and member donations. Many ministries have a desire to support the community but do not have clear vision, resources, or manpower to make a sufficient kingdom impact on communities.
- The concept of being paid for services or paying members for their expertise is often shunned. Volunteer and sacrifice for the sake of the gospel are strongly preached and encouraged. Riches is sometimes discouraged as being poor is seen as a self-sacrificed life.

### Characteristics Of A Fivefold Paradigm

- There is a team mandate of apostles, prophets, evangelists, pastors, teachers who unify and work together to establish and advance the kingdom of God.
- The team operates as vision carriers who utilize their giftings and callings to govern and guide the members, the vision, the climate and culture of the ministry, the atmosphere, the community, and the region.
- The team is trained in their gifts, destiny and calling so they can train others; they are also equipped and released in their life's vision as an extension of the fivefold paradigm and the body of Christ.
- Members are also identified, trained, equipped, licensed, ordained, mentored, parented, counseled, coached, released, and covered as they operate in ministry, works of service within the ministry and the community, and as they journey in their gifts, destiny, calling, and life's vision.
- There is a building up, perfecting, maturing of the soul, mind, body, spirit, and identity of members, so they can be effectively discipled and transformed, with the ability to demonstrate continual growth and maturity as believers of God.
- Being created, grounded, secure in the increasing personal relationship, knowledge, and faith of God, the Bible, sound doctrine, Jesus, the Holy Spirit, and God's kingdom, is constantly taught and practiced where full maturity is a tangible lifestyle.
- Members are taught how to hear God for themselves, study the word, and spiritually empower and mature their own destiny, callings, and life visions.
- Continual fellowship, covenant, and unconditional love is taught, encouraged, and practiced to mature the saints to be able to stand in the face of the challenges and deceits of the world.
- Discipling believers in continual growth with an ever increasing outward manifestation of love is exercised to establish a complete unity in the faith and of the knowledge of the Son of God, and being a son of God.

---

*The team is trained in their gifts, destiny and calling so they can train others*

---

- Members are equipped to withstand life challenges, hardships, persecution, warfare, and to be offensive in warfare tactics and healthy living to avoid unnecessary trials and tribulations.
- There is a divine emphasis on marriage and family and walking together in destiny and fivefold equipping and empowerment. Spouses and family members come alongside of the leader as vision carriers to help support and advance the vision. Depending on the personality of the leader, sometimes the ministry can be placed ahead of marriages and families, but this is often discouraged. There is greater emphasis and balance on taking rest days, vacations, time with family, and prioritizing marriage and family over the vision. Many healthy fivefold leaders believe the vision begins at home first, and as the leader takes care of the home, they are demonstrating the balance and effectiveness of healthy fivefold ministry as ministry begins with family.
- Greater works of deliverance – essentially the casting out of devils, healings, miracles, signs, wonders, living and operating through the supernatural is taught, encouraged and tangible in the members, ministry, and transferable as they minister and empower other believers and ministries.
- Services and trainings can occur at anytime or date and are usually nontraditional, and God led. Fivefold members are taught to live a lifestyle in God where services and trainings are part of their growth rather than a choice to which they fit into their schedule.
- Ministries can be housed in homes, schools, hotels, community center, etc., and is usually operated more as a movement than a traditional church. Recently revival hubs and centers are being established to house fivefold ministries. Ministers have also become cleaver in having pop up services in various places such as parks, beaches, parking lots, building sites or collaborating with businesses or other ministries to partner in conducting services.
- Unique individual fivefold blueprints that are God designed, God imaged, and God-ordained, aide in nullifying religion and tradition while keeping the kingdom of God SHIFTING, moving, and advancing in the earth.
- Weighty tangible glory, open heavens, the combatting of principalities, territorial spirits, powers, ruler spirits, spiritual wickedness in high places, and fervently impacting and overtaking land, communities, regions, and nations, thrusts the members and the fivefold vision into

pursuing the fullness of the gospel of Jesus Christ and all salvation encompasses.
- Ministry is not confined to the four walls of the church as revival reformation is foundational to fivefold ministry. Ministry is not just about worship services but establishing and building homes, schools, ministries, programs, organizations, hospitals, banks, businesses, etc. Infiltrating world systems (e.g. family, governmental, educational, business, arts & entertainment, media, religion), with the kingdom of God and establishing God's kingdom in communities, regions, and nations to draw people out of the world's system is an essential mandate of the fivefold paradigm. Revival reformation is used to create limitless streams of income to sustain the ministry, the members, assist the poor, widows, and needy while advancing the kingdom in communities, regions, and nations.
- Riches and seeking ways to produce finances are encouraged to be examples of godly prosperity, demonstrating responsibility over gifts, talents, callings, and the works of thine hands, and to further position self to advance the kingdom.
- Challenging and exposing error, false doctrine, false fivefold ministers, and idolatry is also part of releasing sound doctrine and godly truths into the earth.
- A generational mandate is upon the ministry where successors are set and equipped to carry the vision from generation to generation.

### *Homework Explorations:*
1. Journal five distinct difference between the pastoral and fivefold ministry paradigm.
2. As you consider this chapter, journal where you would need to SHIFT to posture fully into a fivefold ministry paradigm.
3. As you consider the concepts of religious doctrines, how have they impacted the body of Christ from operating in a true fivefold ministry paradigm?
4. What are your thoughts about ministry infiltrating world and demonic systems, and establishing kingdom businesses, organizations, centers in communities and regions?
5. Write a paper on a kingdom business, organization, etc., that you believe is needed in your region. Discuss how you would establish it and how it would impact the people and region as a whole.

# OFFICE OF FIVEFOLD MINISTRY

Dictionary.com defines *office* as:
1. a position of employment, duty, trust, or authority, especially in the government
2. a corporation, a society, or the like

Dictionary.com defines *officer* as:
1. a person who holds a position of rank or authority in the army, navy, air force, or any similar organization, especially one who holds a commission
2. a member of a police department or a constable
3. a person licensed to take full or partial responsibility for the operation of a merchant ship or other large civilian ship; a master or mate
4. a person appointed or elected to some position of responsibility or authority in the government, a corporation, a society, etc.
5. (in some honorary orders) a member of any rank except the lowest

*Thoughts to consider:*
- Duties and authority of officers may vary according to rank.
- Duties and authority can also vary according to specific a calling and divine specialty.
- Some officers mature into being generals or pillars of the faith. A general is able to demonstrate, train, equip, officiate, and command all operations of their office with long-standing integrity, excellence, and tangible success.
- Officers are not self-appointed. They are called and set apart by God and commissioned by a called, set apart, commissioned, responsible, trained, equipped, mature officer, usually of higher or equal ranking. Apostle Paul was set apart originally by Jesus Christ (**Romans 1:1, 1Corinthians 1:1**); he eventually met with the other apostles who walked directly with Jesus, and was extended the right hand of fellowship which was an act of supporting that he was a true apostle who was equipped to operate in the calling and mandate upon his life (**Study Galatians 2**).

God will often unction an officer to go to delegated authorities and companies to be trained, equipped, confirmed, and/or set apart.

> ***Galatians 2:2 The Amplified Bible*** *I went because it was specially and divinely revealed to me that I should go, and I put before them the Gospel [declaring to them that] which I preach among the Gentiles. However, [I presented the matter] privately before those of repute, [for I wanted to make*

*certain, by thus at first confining my communication to this private conference] that I was not running or had not run in vain [guarding against being discredited either in what I was planning to do or had already done].*

*It is important to be directed by God because all who say they are fivefold are not. Being set apart by a false brethren taints your gift and calling.*

***Galatians 2:4-5 The Amplified Bible*** *[My precaution was] because of false brethren who had been secretly smuggled in [to the Christian brotherhood]; they had slipped in to spy on our liberty and the freedom which we have in Christ Jesus, that they might again bring us into bondage [under the Law of Moses]. To them we did not yield submission even for a moment, that the truth of the Gospel might continue to be [preserved] for you [in its purity].*

Sometimes training and equipping will be required, and sometimes hands-on training with God will be sufficient. This is the reason it is important for the prospective officer to be God led to those who are to commission them in their office. They will not make the candidate unnecessarily prove their expertise. They will see the expertise the candidate already has and will only require training and equipping where necessary as God leads.

***Galatians 2:6-8 The Amplified Bible*** *Moreover, [no new requirements were made] by those who were reputed to be something – though what was their individual position and whether they really were of importance or not makes no difference to me; God is not impressed with the positions that men hold and He is not partial and recognizes no external distinctions – those [I say] who were of repute imposed no new requirements upon me [had nothing to add to my Gospel, and from them I received no new suggestions]. But on the contrary, when they [really] saw that I had been entrusted [to carry] the Gospel to the uncircumcised [Gentiles, just as definitely] as Peter had been entrusted [to proclaim] the Gospel to the circumcised [Jews, they were agreeable]; For He Who motivated and fitted Peter and worked effectively through him for the mission to the circumcised, motivated and fitted me and worked through me also for [the mission to] the Gentiles.*

*Officers are not self-appointed.*

Commissioning occurs when it is clearly perceived, recognized, and understood that the candidate is ready to walk in the office to which they have been called.

> ***Galatians 2:9-10 The Amplified Bible*** *And when they knew (perceived, recognized, understood, and acknowledged) the grace (God's unmerited favor and spiritual blessing) that had been bestowed upon me, James and Cephas (Peter) and John, who were reputed to be pillars of the Jerusalem church, gave to me and Barnabas the right hand of fellowship, with the understanding that we should go to the Gentiles and they to the circumcised (Jews). They only [made one stipulation], that we were to remember the poor, which very thing I was also eager to do.*

Often we are already operating in a measure of our calling before being trained and equipped. Thus it requires humility to subject ourselves to training and equipping because we have already been doing the works. Works, however, do not demonstrate that we clearly perceive, understand, and acknowledge the office we have been called to. This must be demonstrated not just in works but understanding the definition, purpose, and function of the call. Paul had a specialized apostleship to the uncircumcised but was able to still demonstrate that his training and equipping was the same as Peter who was an apostolic pillar that walked with and was physically commission and set apart by Jesus. This is key. There is no such thing as an almost officer. Officers must be equipped in fullness, not measure.

> ***Galatians 2:6-10*** *But of these who seemed to be somewhat, (whatsoever they were, it maketh no matter to me: God accepteth no man's person:) for they who seemed to be somewhat in conference added nothing to me: But contrariwise, when they saw that the gospel of the uncircumcision was committed unto me, as the gospel of the circumcision was unto Peter; (For he that wrought effectually in Peter to the apostleship of the circumcision, the same was mighty in me toward the Gentiles:) And when James, Cephas, and John, who seemed to be pillars, perceived the grace that was given unto me, they gave to me and Barnabas the right hands of fellowship; that we should go unto the heathen, and they unto the circumcision. Only they would that we should remember the poor; the same which I also was forward to do.*

Most are identified in their office by God then need training, definition, and equipping to fully understand their calling. Submitting to training and equipping is essential to walking successfully in destiny and calling. It lessens, the warfare, mistakes, having to uproot ungodly fruit and faulty foundations, and redoing seasons of trials and testings.

Many become excited about the revealing of the office and the title and want to bypass equipping.

Many get caught up in prophetic words and the love of being validated and fail to discern that some prophecies have to be worked and processed into in order to come to pass, and validation is simply fleeting empowerment of potential that only becomes a reality when training and equipping occurs.

Many assume works, signs, and wonders validate that they are ready for the office. But the office is more than just ministry, labor, and gift manifestations. This is the work of a believer, but not necessarily the government of the office.

Some officer duties include:

- Leading platoons (e.g., a company or groups of people, a military unit, team, headquarters).
- Counseling and mentoring people and releasing and journeying with them in their destiny and calling.
- Teaching, training, and equipping new, low ranking, or specialized officers, or groups of people that God has charged oversight to.
- Incur the maintenance, integration, management, and administration of the office.
- Commanding troops during war.
- Sustaining and maintaining critical military operations.
- Contending against high ranking demonic and or wicked officers.
- Overseeing ministries, market place, and business arenas, social and community organizations, and political or economic liaisons.
- Overseeing communities, regions, or nations.

When one is the office, all authority is given unto them in heaven and in earth.

> ***Matthew 18:16*** *Then the eleven disciples went away into Galilee, into a mountain where Jesus had appointed them. And when they saw him, they worshipped him: but some doubted. And Jesus came and spake unto them, saying, All power is given unto me in heaven and in earth.*

This means the officer's authority is without measure. They have been ordained by God to reign and rule in both spheres such that the kingdom of God is evident in all they set their hands to do. SHIFT!

## *Homework Explorations:*
1. As you consider this chapter, what is the difference between the authority of a regular believer and one who holds and office?
2. Journal your thoughts on how religious and traditional doctrines have stifled the authority of fivefold officers.
3. Google an officer in the Marines, Navy, Army, or Airforce. Journal their characteristics and duties. Journal the similarities and differences to the officers in the body of Christ.

# KINGDOM OFFICER JOURNAL ASSIGNMENT

*The US Army News & Information* website *(https://www.army.mil)* lists the core values and creeds of an officer of the United States Army. **All the Information listed in this chapter is from that website.** As you study them, spend time exploring and journaling what they would mean as an officer in the kingdom of God. Journal your thoughts and perceptions in DETAIL as it relates to your office or your perception of the person in the fivefold office.

## ARMY CORE VALUES

### Loyalty
Bear true faith and allegiance to the U.S. Constitution, the Army, your unit, and other Soldiers. Bearing true faith and allegiance is a matter of believing in and devoting yourself to something or someone. A loyal Soldier is one who supports the leadership and stands up for fellow Soldiers. By wearing the uniform of the U.S. Army, you are expressing your loyalty. And by doing your share, you show your loyalty to your unit.

### Duty
Fulfill your obligations. Doing your duty means more than carrying out your assigned tasks. Duty means being able to accomplish tasks as part of a team. The work of the U.S. Army is a
Many people know what the words Loyalty, Duty, Respect, Selfless Service, Honor, Integrity, and Personal Courage mean. But how often do you see someone actually live up to them? Soldiers learn these values in detail during Basic Combat Training (BCT), from then on they live them every day in everything they do — whether they're on the job or off. In short, the Seven Core Army Values listed below are what being a Soldier all is about.

A complex combination of missions, tasks, and responsibilities — all in constant motion. Our work entails building one assignment onto another. You fulfill your obligations as a part of your unit every time you resist the temptation to take "shortcuts" that might undermine the integrity of the final product.

## Respect

Treat people as they should be treated. In the Soldier's Code, we pledge to "treat others with dignity and respect while expecting others to do the same." Respect is what allows us to appreciate the best in other people. Respect is trusting that all people have done their jobs and fulfilled their duty. And self-respect is a vital ingredient with the Army value of respect, which results from knowing you have put forth your best effort. The Army is one team, and each of us has something to contribute.

## Selfless Service

Put the welfare of the nation, the Army, and your subordinates before your own. Selfless service is larger than just one person. In serving your country, you are doing your duty loyally without thought of recognition or gain. The basic building block of selfless service is the commitment of each team member to go a little further, endure a little longer, and look a little closer to see how he or she can add to the effort.

## Honor

Live up to Army values. The nation's highest military award is The Medal of Honor. This award goes to Soldiers who make honor a matter of daily living — Soldiers who develop the habit of being honorable and solidify that habit with every value choice they make. Honor is a matter of carrying out, acting, and living the values of respect, duty, loyalty, selfless service, integrity, and personal courage in everything you do.

## Integrity

Do what's right, legally and morally. Integrity is a quality you develop by adhering to moral principles. It requires that you do and say nothing that deceives others. As your integrity grows, so does the trust others place in you. The more choices you make based on integrity, the more this highly prized value will affect your relationships with family and friends, and, finally, the fundamental acceptance of yourself.

## Personal Courage

Face fear, danger or adversity (physical or moral). Personal courage has long been associated with our Army. With physical courage, it is a matter of enduring physical duress and at times risking personal safety. Facing moral fear or adversity may be a long, slow process of continuing forward on the right path, especially if taking those actions is not popular with others. You can build your personal courage by daily standing up for and acting upon the things that you know are honorable.

## OATH OF ENLISTMENT

I, _____, do solemnly swear (or affirm) that I will support and defend the Constitution of the United States against all enemies, foreign and domestic; that I will bear true faith and allegiance to the same; and that I will obey the orders of the President of the United States and the orders of the officers appointed over me, according to regulations and the Uniform Code of Military Justice. So help me God." (Title 10, US Code; Act of 5 May 1960 replacing the wording first adopted in 1789, with amendment effective 5 October 1962).

## OATH OF COMMISSIONED OFFICERS

I ___, do solemnly swear (or affirm) that I will support and defend the Constitution of the United States against all enemies, foreign and domestic; that I will bear true faith and allegiance to the same; that I take this obligation freely, without any mental reservation or purpose of evasion; and that I will well and faithfully discharge the duties of the office on which I am about to enter. So help me God. (Title 5 U.S. Code 3331, an individual, except the President, elected or appointed to an office of honor or profit in the civil service or uniformed services)

## WARRIORS ETHOS

- I will always place the mission first.
- I will never accept defeat.
- I will never quit.
- I will never leave a fallen comrade.

## SOLDIER'S CREED

- I am an American Soldier.
- I am a warrior and a member of a team.
- I serve the people of the United States, and live the Army Values.
- I will always place the mission first.
- I will never accept defeat.
- I will never quit.
- I will never leave a fallen comrade.
- I am disciplined, physically, and mentally tough, trained, and proficient in my warrior tasks and drills.
- I always maintain my arms, my equipment, and myself.

- I am an expert, and I am a professional.
- I stand ready to deploy, engage, and destroy, the enemies of the United States of America in close combat.
- I am a guardian of freedom and the American way of life.
- I am an American Soldier.

## ARMY CADET SONG

- I am an Army cadet.
- Soon I will take an oath to become an Army officer. Committed to defending the values which makes this nation great.
- Honor is my touchstone.
- I understand mission first and people always.
- I am the past, the spirit of those warriors who have made the final sacrifice.
- I am the present, the scholar and apprentice soldier enhancing my skills in the science of warfare and the art of leadership.
- But above all I am the future, the future warrior leader of the United States Army.
- May God give me the compassion and judgment to lead and the gallantry in battle to win.
- I will do my duty.

### *Homework Explorations:*
1. Journal your thoughts and perceptions in DETAIL regarding this chapter as it relates to your office or your perception of person in the fivefold office.
2. Spend time singing the Army Cadet Song over yourself and asking God to empower you in a greater fashion as his officer.

# ALLEGIANCE OF A KINGDOM OFFICER

Like the United States Army, the kingdom of God has core values and creeds for its officers. Once you become a fivefold officer, your allegiance is to the kingdom of God. Your life is no longer your own. Every decision you make, even personally, impacts and should align with the kingdom's mandate and government. As an officer, you are an ambassador and a literal representation of God chosen to govern and establish God's kingdom in the earth. You represent the office and at no time do you get to dishonor the values, creeds, oaths, or warriors' code.

> *As an officer, you are an ambassador and a literal representation of God chosen to govern and establish God's kingdom in the earth*

## THE KINGDOM'S CONSTITUTION – THE HOLY BIBLE

*2Timothy 2:17 Do your best to present yourself to God as one approved, a worker who does not need to be ashamed and who correctly handles the word of truth.*

## KINGDOM VALUES

### Submitted To God

*Romans 13:1 Let every soul be subject unto the higher powers. For there is no power but of God: the powers that be are ordained of God.*

### Imitators is God & His Love

*John 13:34-35 So now I am giving you a new commandment: Love each other. Just as I have loved you, you should love each other. Your love for one another will prove to the world that you are my disciples.*

*Ephesians 4:2 Be completely humble and gentle; be patient, bearing with one another in love.*

*Ephesians 5:1-2 The Amplified Bible THEREFORE BE imitators of God [copy Him and follow His example], as well-beloved children [imitate their father]. And walk in love, [esteeming and delighting in one another] as Christ loved us and gave Himself up for us, slain offering and sacrifice to God [for you, so that it became] a sweet fragrance.*

***1Peter 4:8*** *Above all, love each other deeply, because love covers over a multitude of sins.*

## Servant's Heart

***Matthew 23:11*** *The greatest among you must be a servant.*

***Mark 10:45*** *For even the Son of Man did not come to be served, but to serve, and to give His life a ransom for many.*

***Philippians 2:5-8*** *Have this attitude in yourselves which was also in Christ Jesus, who, although He existed in the form of God, did not regard equality with God a thing to be grasped, but emptied Himself, taking the form of a bond-servant, and being made in the likeness of men.*

## Selflessly Esteem Others

***Philippians 2:3-4 The Amplified Bible*** *Do nothing from factional motives [through contentiousness, strife, selfishness, or for unworthy ends] or prompted by conceit and empty arrogance. Instead, in the true spirit of humility (lowliness of mind) let each regard the others as better than and superior to himself [thinking more highly of one another than you do of yourselves]. Let each of you esteem and look upon and be concerned for not [merely] his own interests, but also each for the interests of others.*

## Humble, Meek, Long Suffering, Peace Seekers, Unity Makers

***Ephesians 4:1-3*** *I therefore, the prisoner of the Lord, beseech you that ye walk worthy of the vocation wherewith ye are called, With all lowliness and meekness, with longsuffering, forbearing one another in love; Endeavouring to keep the unity of the Spirit in the bond of peace.*

***Philippians 2:5*** *Let this same attitude and purpose and [humble] mind be in you which was in Christ Jesus: [Let Him be your example in humility:]*

## Full of & Surrendered To The Holy Spirit

***John 14:16-17*** *I will ask the Father, and he will give you another Helper to be with you forever – the Spirit of truth. The world cannot accept him,* *because it does not see him or know him. But you know him, because he lives with you and he will be in you.*

**John 16:13** *Howbeit when he, the Spirit of truth, is come, he will guide you into all truth: for he shall not speak of himself; but whatsoever he shall hear, that shall he speak: and he will shew you things to come.*

**Luke 24:49** *And, behold, I send the promise of my Father upon you: but tarry ye in the city of Jerusalem, until ye be endued with power from on high.*

**Acts 13:52** *And the disciples were continually filled with joy and with the Holy Spirit.*

## Governed By The Word Of God

**John 8:31-32** *Then Jesus said to those Jews who believed Him, "If you abide in My word, you are My disciples indeed. And you shall know the truth, and the truth shall make you free."*

## Life of Purity & Holiness

**1Peter 1:15-16** *But just as he who called you is holy, so be holy in all you do; for it is written: "Be holy, because I am holy."*

**Titus 1:15-16 The Amplified Bible** *To the pure [in heart and conscience] all things are pure, but to the defiled and corrupt and unbelieving nothing is pure; their very minds and consciences are defiled and polluted. They profess to know God [to recognize, perceive, and be acquainted with Him], but deny and disown and renounce Him by what they do; they are detestable and* loathsome, unbelieving and disobedient and disloyal and rebellious, and [they are] unfit and worthless for good work (deed or enterprise) of any kind.

## Righteous

**Romans 8:4 The Amplified Bible** *So that the righteous and just requirement of the Law might be fully met in us who live and move not in the ways of the flesh but in the ways of the Spirit [our lives governed not by the standards and according to the dictates of the flesh, but controlled by the Holy Spirit].*

**Philippians 1:11** *Being filled with the fruits of righteousness, which are by Jesus Christ, unto the glory and praise of God.*

*James 1:4* But let patience have [her] perfect work, that ye may be perfect and entire, wanting nothing.

## Faithful

*Matthew 25:45-47* Who then is a faithful and wise servant, whom his lord hath made ruler over his household, to give them meat in due season? Blessed is that servant, whom his lord when he cometh shall find so doing. Verily I say unto you, That he shall make him ruler over all his goods.

*Matthew 25:21* His lord said to him, Well done, good and faithful servant; you were faithful over a few things, I will make you ruler over many things. Enter into the joy of your lord.

*1Corinthians 4:2* Moreover it is required in stewards that one be found faithful.

## Teachable

*Acts 2:42* They spent their time learning from the apostles, and they were like family to each other. They also broke bread and prayed together.

## Violent Warrior

*Matthew 11:12* And from the days of John the Baptist until now the kingdom of heaven suffereth violence, and the violent take it by force.

## Powerful

*Luke 10:9* Behold, I give unto you power to tread on serpents and scorpions, and over all the power of the enemy: and nothing shall by any means hurt you.

*Mark 16:18* They shall take up serpents; and if they drink any deadly thing, it shall not hurt them; they shall lay hands on the sick, and they shall recover.

## Key Holders

*Matthew 16:19* And I will give unto thee the keys of the kingdom of heaven: and whatsoever thou shalt bind on earth shall be bound in heaven: and whatsoever thou shalt loose on earth shall be loosed in heaven.

*Matthew 18:18* Truly I tell you, whatever you forbid and declare to be improper and unlawful on earth must be what is already forbidden in *heaven, and whatever you permit and declare proper and lawful on earth must be what is already permitted in heaven.*

## Triumphant Against Adversity

***2Corinthians 4:7-12 The Amplified Bible** However, we possess this precious treasure [the divine Light of the Gospel] in [frail, human] vessels of earth, that the grandeur and exceeding greatness of the power may be shown to be from God and not from ourselves. We are hedged in (pressed) on every side [troubled and oppressed in every way], but not cramped or crushed; we suffer embarrassments and are perplexed and unable to find a way out, but not driven to despair; We are pursued (persecuted and hard driven), but not deserted [to stand alone]; we are struck down to the ground, but never struck out and destroyed; Always carrying about in the body the liability and exposure to the same putting to death that the Lord Jesus suffered, so that the [resurrection] life of Jesus also may be shown forth by and in our bodies. For we who live are constantly [experiencing] being handed over to death for Jesus' sake, that the [resurrection] life of Jesus also may be evidenced through our flesh which is liable to death. Thus death is actively at work in us, but [it is in order that our] life [may be actively at work] in you.*

***1Corinthians 13:7** Beareth all things, believeth all things, hopeth all things, endureth all things.*

## Perfecters, Equippers, Edifiers

***Ephesians 4:11-12** And he gave some, apostles; and some, prophets; and some, evangelists; and some, pastors and teachers; For the perfecting of the saints, for the work of the ministry, for the edifying of the body of Christ.*

## Preach with Conviction & Signs Following

***1Thessalonians 1:5** For our [preaching of the] glad tidings (the Gospel) came to you not only in word, but also in [its own inherent] power and in the Holy Spirit and with great conviction and absolute certainty [on our part]. You know what kind of men we proved [ourselves] to be among you for your good.*

OATH OF ENLISTMENT

We enlist as disciples then SHIFT into our offices.

> ***Matthew 10:6-8*** *Do not go in the way of the Gentiles, and do not enter any city of the Samaritans, but rather go to the lost sheep of the house of Israel.; "And as you go, preach, saying, 'The kingdom of heaven is at hand.'; "Heal the sick, raise the dead, cleanse the lepers, cast out demons. Freely you received, freely give.*
>
> ***John 15:16*** *You did not choose me, but I chose you and appointed you so that you might go and bear fruit – fruit that will last – and so that whatever you ask in my name the Father will give you.*

As an officer of the Kingdom of God, I _____ enlist in the army of the Lord. I enlist sacrificing myself so that his kingdom may eternally advance in the earth. I will preach the unadulterated gospel of Jesus Christ and his kingdom, while healing the sick, raising the dead, cleansing the lepers, casting out demons, freely giving what I have received. I recognize that I am chosen and appointed to bear lasting fruit of God and his kingdom. My life is not my own but is about God and the government of his kingdom.

## GREAT OATH OF COMMISSIONED OFFICERS

> ***Matthew 28:16-20 The Amplified Bible*** *Now the eleven disciples went to Galilee, to the mountain to which Jesus had directed and made appointment with them. And when they saw Him, they fell down and worshiped Him; but some doubted. Jesus approached and, breaking the silence, said to them, All authority (all power of rule) in heaven and on earth has been given to Me. Go then and make disciples of all the nations, baptizing the into the name of the Father and of the Son and of the Holy Spirit, Teaching them to observe everything that I have commanded you, and behold, I am with you all the days (perpetually, uniformly, and on every occasion), to the [very] close and consummation of the age. Amen (so let it be).*
>
> ***Mark 16:15*** *He said to them, 'Go into all the world and preach the gospel to all creation.'*
>
> ***Ephesians 4:1-6*** *I therefore, the prisoner of the Lord, beseech you that ye walk worthy of the vocation wherewith ye are called, With all lowliness and meekness, with longsuffering, forbearing one another in love; Endeavouring to keep the unity of the Spirit in the bond of peace. There is one body, and one Spirit, even as ye are called in one hope of your calling;*

*One Lord, one faith, one baptism, One God and Father of all, who is above all, and through all, and in you all.*

***Ephesians 4:11-16*** *And he gave some, apostles; and some, prophets; and some, evangelists; and some, pastors and teachers; For the perfecting of the saints, for the work of the ministry, for the edifying of the body of Christ: Till we all come in the unity of the faith, and of the knowledge of the Son of God, unto a perfect man, unto the measure of the stature of the fulness of Christ: That we henceforth be no more children, tossed to and fro, and carried about with every wind of doctrine, by the sleight of men, and cunning craftiness, whereby they lie in wait to deceive; But speaking the truth in love, may grow up into him in all things, which is the head, even Christ: From whom the whole body fitly joined together and compacted by that which every joint supplieth, according to the effectual working in the measure of every part, maketh increase of the body unto the edifying of itself in love.*

As an officer, I _____ am a gift to the body of Christ and the world at large. As a gift my life is not my own. I belong to Jesus Christ and the people he has given me to for the building of their lives and callings and the advancement of the kingdom of God in the earth. I am merely a part of the body of Christ, fitly joined together, so that the body of Christ can be advanced in its fullness. All authority (all power of rule) in heaven and on earth has been given to me to GO FORTH, preach and make disciples of all the nations; baptizing them into the name of the Father and of the Son and of the Holy Spirit, and teaching them all I know about Jesus Christ and his kingdom.

## WARRIORS ETHOS

***2Timothy 3-7*** *Thou therefore endure hardness, as a good soldier of Jesus Christ. No man that warreth entangleth himself with the affairs of this life; that he may please him who hath chosen him to be a soldier. And if a man also strive for masteries, yet is he not crowned, except he strive lawfully. The husbandman that laboureth must be first partaker of the fruits. Consider what I say; and the Lord give thee understanding in all things.*

A good soldier is a champion for the cause of Jesus Christ

<u>Warreth</u> means <u>*strateuomai*</u> in Greek and means:
1. to serve in a military campaign; figuratively

2. to execute the apostolate (with its arduous duties and functions)
3. to contend with carnal inclinations: — soldier, (go to) war(-fare)
4. to make a military expedition, to lead soldiers to war or to battle
5. (spoken of a commander) to do military duty, be on active service
6. be a soldier, to fight

> ***The Message Versions 3-7*** *When the going gets rough, take it on the chin with the rest of us, the way Jesus did. A soldier on duty doesn't get caught up in making deals at the marketplace. He concentrates on carrying out orders. An athlete who refuses to play by the rules will never get anywhere. It's the diligent farmer who gets the produce. Think it over. God will make it all plain.*

I _____ am an officer in the army of the Lord, enduring hardness as a good soldier of Jesus Christ. I do not entangle myself with the affairs of this life, for my life as a chosen officer is to please God. I do not just give the cup of destiny to others; I drink the full cup so that I may be a partake of the percussions and fruit of Jesus Christ and his kingdom. I govern his kingdom as I preach. I judge, annihilate, and overthrow darkness as I preach. I contend against any and everything that contends against God and his kingdom. For I serve in a military office, execute God's apostolic mandate, duties, and functions, make military expeditions, lead soldiers to war, and manifest the victory of Jesus Christ that was already won through the cross.

## WARRIORS CREED

***2Corinthians 10:3-4*** *For though we walk in the flesh, we do not war after the flesh: (For the weapons of our warfare are not carnal, but mighty through God to the pulling down of strong holds).*

<u>Warfare</u> is *strateia* in Greek and means:
1. military service, i.e. (figuratively) the apostolic career (as one of hardship and danger)
2. warfare, an expedition, campaign, military service, warfare
3. metaph. Paul likens his contest with the difficulties that oppose him in the discharge of his apostolic duties, as warfare

> ***Ephesians 6:10-20*** *Finally, my brethren, be strong in the Lord, and in the power of his might. Put on the whole armour of God, that ye may be able to stand against the wiles of the devil. For we wrestle not against*

*flesh and blood, but against principalities, against powers, against the rulers of the darkness of this world, against spiritual wickedness in high places. Wherefore take unto you the whole armour of God, that ye may be able to withstand in the evil day, and having done all, to stand.*
*Stand therefore, having your loins girt about with truth, and having on the breastplate of righteousness; And your feet shod with the preparation of the gospel of peace; Above all, taking the shield of faith, wherewith ye shall be able to quench all the fiery darts of the wicked. And take the helmet of salvation, and the sword of the Spirit, which is the word of God: Praying always with all prayer and supplication in the Spirit, and watching thereunto with all perseverance and supplication for all saints; And for me, that utterance may be given unto me, that I may open my mouth boldly, to* make known the mystery of the *gospel, For which I am an ambassador in bonds: that therein I may speak boldly, as I ought to speak.*

- I do not walk or war in the flesh but through the power and authority of my spirit and my governmental office.
- I am a military kingdom officer as this is my apostolic career.
- I am a warrior and a member of a mighty violent, glory carrying team.
- I serve the people for I am a sold out, chosen gift, and live selflessly through my kingdom's values.
- I will always place the mission first even in the face of hardship and danger.
- I will never accept defeat.
- I will never quit.
- I esteem others higher than myself and I will never leave a fallen comrade.
- I am disciplined, spiritually, physically and mentally tough, trained, and proficient in my warrior tasks and drills.
- I always maintain my mantle, my armor, my equipment, and myself.
- I am an unwavering mouthpiece of God boldly making known the mysteries of the gospel of the kingdom for which I am an ambassador in bonds.
- I am fully armored in my stance and weaponry.
- I have on the helmet of salvation, breastplate of righteousness, shield of faith, girded with loins of truth, shod my feet with the gospel of peace.
- I am surrounded in the light and glory of the Lord.
- I am an expert in my office, and I am a professional.

- ❖ I stand ready to deploy troops, and to engage, and destroy principalities, powers, rulers of the darkness of this world, against spiritual wickedness in high places, and enemies of the kingdom of God in close combat.
- ❖ I am a guardian of freedom and the kingdom way of life.
- ❖ I am a kingdom officer.

### *Homework Explorations:*

1. As you studied and considered the revelation in this chapter, journal in detail what you learned regarding the values, codes, and creeds of being a fivefold officer.
2. Examine areas of your character and nature that needs to be cultivated. Ask God for revelation on how to strengthen these attributes in your life.
3. Examine areas where you need to strengthen as a warring officer in God. Ask God for revelation on how to embrace warfare as a lifestyle and how to assert your authority over demonic and worldly forces.
4. Write a song regarding you being commissioned in the army of the Lord.

# FIVEFOLD OFFICE OPERATIONS

Let's explore the fivefold positions and how operating in the fivefold edifies the body while SHIFTING atmospheres and people, thus awakening bringing forth the presence and wonders of God.

## FIVEFOLD SCRIPTURAL FOUNDATION

> ***Ephesians 4:11-12*** *The Amplified Version And His gifts were varied; He Himself appointed and gave men to us, some to be apostles (special messengers), some prophets (inspired preachers and expounders), some evangelists (preachers of the Gospel, traveling missionaries), some pastors (shepherds of His flock) and teachers. His intention was the perfecting and the full equipping of the saints (His consecrated people), that they should do the work of ministering toward building up Christ's body (the church).*
>
> ***The Message Bible*** *He handed out gifts above and below, filled heaven with his gifts, filled earth with his gifts. He handed out gifts of apostle, prophet, evangelist, and pastor-teacher to train Christ's followers in skilled servant work, working within Christ's body, the church, until we're all moving rhythmically and easily with each other, efficient and graceful in response to God's Son, fully mature adults, fully developed within and without, fully alive like Christ.*

This passage of scripture presents the relevancy of purpose for Jesus, giving the gifts of the fivefold offices to the church. Jesus never took these gifts away. He would never give a gift then take it back. These gifts are just as important today as they were over 2,000 years ago. When Jesus gave these gifted offices it was for:

- ✓ The perfecting and maturing of God's people, his church, the community, lands, and regions
- ✓ The work and equipping of the ministry where the church and the world would come to God for assistance and supply of their needs and desires.
- ✓ The edifying, empowering, building up of the Body of Christ.

This was to be continual until solidification:

- ✓ In the faith and of the knowledge of the Son of God was evident.
- ✓ Of the full maturity and growth in the Lord was a tangible lifestyle.
- ✓ Where all reached the full measure of the stature of Christ.

This mandate reveals that fivefold ministry is never-ending. It is the purpose of God for the saints and for his church. It is the revival reformation that we are to be manifesting, releasing, and establishing in the earth. SHIFT!

God installs these offices in his chosen at birth. If he does not install this office in you, you cannot promote yourself to this office or go to a Christian school, learn these gifts, then be positioned into these offices. Either they are in you or they are not. Either they are part of your destiny and calling or not. These offices are for the purposes of providing spiritual authorities that can empower, equip, and release the body of Christ in their giftings and callings while asserting and maintaining Godly jurisdiction against principalities and strongholds that would strive to bind people, lands, and regions. A person can be apostolic, prophetic, evangelistic, etc., but not operate in a governmental office. The office provides the officer the ability to govern and legislate against demonic entities, spiritual realms, regions, and within the constructs of assemblies, businesses, and communities. If God has not called you to this, you can encounter a lot of hardship and tribulation by putting yourself in these positions as those who have the offices, have a grace to contend and endure the warfare that comes with these offices.

> ***2Corinthians 4:8-17*** *We are troubled on every side, yet not distressed; we are perplexed, but not in despair; Persecuted, but not forsaken; cast down, but not destroyed; Always bearing about in the body the dying of the Lord Jesus, that the life also of Jesus might be made manifest in our body. For we which live are always delivered unto death for Jesus' sake, that the life also of Jesus might be made manifest in our mortal flesh. So then death worketh in us, but life in you. We having the same spirit of faith, according as it is written, I believed, and therefore have I spoken; we also believe, and therefore speak; Knowing that he which raised up the Lord Jesus shall raise up us also by Jesus, and shall present us with you. For all things are for your sakes, that the abundant grace might through the thanksgiving of many redound to the glory of God. For which cause we faint not; but though our outward man perish, yet the inward man is renewed day by day. For our light affliction, which is but for a moment, worketh for us a far more exceeding and eternal weight of glory; While we look not at the things which are seen, but at the things which are not seen:*

*for the things which are seen are temporal; but the things which are not seen are eternal.*

---

*God installs these offices in his chosen at birth.*

---

Though as saints, we endure some of this for the gospel sake, those in governmental offices live this daily as a lifestyle and mandate. It can be a constant spiritual and natural battle, depending on what season of destiny they are in. Imagine striving to endure this type of lifestyle warfare daily without God, creating you for this position? It would be a horrific life of unnecessary hardship.

I also want to note that if God called you to these offices and you do not embrace them, you can have warfare. The principalities and powers in these jurisdictions are contending and waring for these realms, and you will feel and experience the weight of that whether you embrace your gifted office or not. Your ability to contend and tower in the grace God has given you over these entities is to SHIFT into your rightful office and establish the authority God has given you to govern over darkness within your spheres of influences.

## APOSTLES OFFICE

Some people believe that the office of the apostle died with the apostles in the Bible. If this is true, then my entire ministry, destiny, and calling are a made-up lie. The challenge is you cannot deny the signs and wonders that follow myself and so many other apostles who are efficiently operating in this office in this day and age. There is really no reason for Jesus to take away the gifts of the apostles, but tell us to keep the other four gifts. Notice he said he gave offices as "gifts" in *Ephesians 4*, which means, there was obviously more than the ones in the Bible and would be more as we continue to advance the kingdom. It is a ridiculous theory that does not sufficiently yield solidarity to the foundation of the church, to which Jesus Christ is the chief cornerstone.

> ***Ephesians 2:19-22*** *Now therefore ye are no more strangers and foreigners, but fellow citizens with the saints, and of the household of*

> *God; And are built upon the foundation of the apostles and prophets, Jesus Christ himself being the chief corner stone; In whom all the building fitly framed together groweth unto an holy temple in the Lord: In whom ye also are builded together for an habitation of God through the Spirit.*

People want to exclude women from being apostles, but the scripture clearly identifies female apostles.

> ***Romans 16:7*** *Salute Andronicus and Junia, my kinsmen, and my fellow prisoners, who are of note among the apostles, who also were in Christ before me.*

Jesus had twelve apostles, and one was a betraying devil, yet he was not diminished in his position as an apostle. Jesus trained and equipped him just like he did the other apostles. He gave him ample opportunity to achieve destiny, be exposed for sin issues, in hopes of repenting and turning from his wicked ways.

Yet in our perceived fivefold ministries we contend we can only have one apostle, one prophet, one evangelist, one pastor, one teacher. We make those who are obvious fivefold officers operate in gifts instead of governmental positions, and make them subject themselves to us in an unscriptural way; especially that apostle role. It is really threatening for some reason to have more than one apostle in a ministry. Just be honest and call this what it is - a pastoral one-man show paradigm. This is not true fivefold ministry. It is fake fivefold rooted in fear, insecurity, and false doctrine. **SHIFT RIGHT NOW! SHIFT!** (Study **Matthew 26-28, Mark 16, Luke 24, John 20**)

Apostles continue the work of apostleship that Jesus and the disciples began in the New Testament. Apostles impose the scriptures and enforce the fivefold mandate that Jesus commissioned with the apostles, and that he instituted after resurrecting from the cross.

- ➢ Jesus is the chief cornerstone of apostleship and first apostle – *Ephesians 2:20*
- ➢ The twelve are the first commissioned apostles ordained by Jesus himself – *Matthew 28:16-20, Revelation 21:14*
- ➢ The apostles' names are documented in the foundation of New Jerusalem – *Revelation 21:14*
- ➢ Each biblical apostle saw Jesus in person including Paul – *1Corinthians 1:9*
- ➢ Proof that modern day apostles are of God is found in *Ephesians 4:11*

<u>Apostle</u> in Greek is *apostolos* and means:
1. a delegate, messenger, one sent forth with orders
2. specifically applied to the twelve apostles of Christ
3. in a broader sense applied to other eminent Christian teachers
   1) of Barnabas
   2) of Timothy and Silvanus

<u>Merriam Webster's Online Dictionary</u> defines *delegate* as:
1. a person acting for another
2. a representative to a convention or conference
3. a representative of a United States territory in the House of Representatives
4. a member of the lower house of the legislature

When going forth under the office of an apostle or an apostolic mandate, you are presiding in the position of a delegator. A delegator is one who goes in the place of another and is a representation of a judicial government that presides over a group of people, nation, state, etc. So essentially, when moving in the apostolic office, the apostle is acquiring orders from the Lord and legislating as and through his essence and presence. The apostle is going forth in His stead as His voice, heart, purpose and mandate, with specific orders to bring His kingdom (government) to pass within the people, ministry, environment, and region.

Because an apostle or one under this mandate is operating as a representation of the Lord, he or she operates as one of dominion, strategically assigned to SHIFT people, ministries, atmospheres, regions, and/or a particular sphere to another dimension and influence in the Lord. Dominion is ultimate authority that is unstoppable. Thus, when operating apostolically, one is specifically assigned a kingly realm of dominion and influence.

Often, we are taught that an apostle or one who operates apostolically is one who starts churches, church movements, or ministries such as missions movements, etc. This is indeed true, yet the apostolic mandate is not limited to just establishing churches and the like. The apostolic mandate:

- ✓ Is one of influence in the spirit and natural realm beyond where the people are and even sometimes beyond where the apostle is spiritually.
- ✓ Is a "knowing" that "this is my assignment" and a level of fearlessness that comes with it.

- ✓ Operates inside the spiritual realms with the ability to continual SHIFT themselves, others, atmospheres, climates, regions, spheres, higher and deeper in the realms of God.
- ✓ Sometimes it feels like the apostle and that which he or she has SHIFTED are inside a bubble or floating above or inside the power and presence of God. I believe this is the dominion that protects and gives influence to the apostle as he or she delegates authority and do the work of the Lord in this position.
- ✓ Commands the attention of its congregation, the demonic, and the spiritual realm.
- ✓ Possesses authority and power that SHIFTS lives, churches, communities, and/or atmospheres.
- ✓ Is one of dominion and prominence; demons and opposition may occur but will have no success over one who is walking in the apostolic office.
- ✓ Declares the voice and judgment of God that plant, plows, uproots, builds, establishes and advances his will in the spirit and/or natural realm. Most often, God will give a specific assignment, and the apostle will know what they are planting, plowing, establishing, etc.
- ✓ Sets a standard for excellence and creates discipled followers of Jesus Christ.
- ✓ SHIFTS believers to higher realms of understanding, belief, and inspiration.
- ✓ Identifies gifts via the power of God that overtakes an atmosphere.
- ✓ Open heavens, birth, ignite and establish revival, re-dig revival wells, and awaken revival reformation in people, ministries, atmospheres, and regions.
- ✓ Produce miracles, signs, and wonders through teaching, preaching, and demonstrating the greater works of God.
- ✓ Breaks down, dismantles, and displace religious and traditional walls and barriers.
- ✓ Brings burdens for nations. Teach how to turn the hearts of nations back to God.
- ✓ Dismantle chief, territorial, and ancient spirits and pull down principalities that may have a city, community, church, or people bound.
  - Chief spirits are stronghold demons that rule and have rank in the demonic kingdom and hold people in bondage to the enemy.
  - Territorial spirits rule over specific geographical locations, such as poverty spirit ruling in poor communities.
  - A principality is when demon princes rule over states, cities, or nations.

In *Acts 16*, Paul and Silas were beaten and thrown in jail for delivering a sorcerer and preaching Jesus.

> ***Verse 16-23*** *And it came to pass, as we went to prayer, a certain damsel possessed with a spirit of divination met us, which brought her masters much gain by soothsaying: The same followed Paul and us, and cried, saying, These men are the servants of the most high God, which shew unto us the way of salvation. And this did she many days. But Paul, being grieved, turned and said to the spirit, I command thee in the name of Jesus Christ to come out of her. And he came out the same hour. And when her masters saw that the hope of their gains was gone, they caught Paul and Silas, and drew them into the marketplace unto the rulers. And brought them to the magistrates, saying, these men, being Jews, do exceedingly trouble our city, And teach customs, which are not lawful for us to receive, neither to observe, being Romans. And the multitude rose up together against them: and the magistrates rent off their clothes, and commanded to beat them. And when they had laid many stripes upon them, they cast them into prison, charging the jailor to keep them safely:*

Paul and Silas were under an apostolic mandate to establish the kingdom of God in that city. They were contending against the laws by preaching Jesus and were establishing God's law in the people and in that sphere of influence. Their workings were so evident that a soothsayer possessed with a spirit of divination acknowledged that they were men of *The Most High God*.

<u>The word *divination* in Greek is *python* and means:</u>
1. in Greek mythology, the name of the Pythian serpent or dragon that dwelt in the region of Pytho at the foot of Parnassus in Phocis, and was said to have guarded the oracle at Delphi and been slain by Apollo
2. a spirit of divination

This was a major principality of idolatry operating in that area. Those participating in divination would go to the soothsayer and pay money to receive psychic words concerning their lives. Paul displaced this principality by casting it out of the damsel. This made her masters upset, and they brought Paul and Silas before the courts and had them beaten and thrown in jail.

Paul and Silas where naturally bonded, but spiritually they were still free to rule in dominion and authority as representatives of the Most High God.

> *Acts 16:26-34 And at midnight Paul and Silas prayed, and sang praises unto God: and the prisoners heard them. And suddenly there was a great earthquake, so that the foundations of the prison were shaken: and immediately all the doors were opened, and every one's bands were loosed. And the keeper of the prison awaking out of his sleep, and seeing the prison doors open, he drew out his sword, and would have killed himself, supposing that the prisoners had been fled. But Paul cried with a loud voice, saying, Do thyself no harm: for we are all here. Then he called for a light, and sprang in, and came trembling, and fell down before Paul and Silas, and brought them out, and said, Sirs, what must I do to be saved? And they said, Believe on the Lord Jesus Christ, and thou shalt be saved, and thy house. And they spake unto him the word of the Lord, and to all that were in his house, and he took them the same hour of the night, and washed their stripes; and was baptized, he and all his, straightway. And when he had brought them into his house, he set meat before them, and rejoiced, believing in God with all his house.*

Paul and Silas were apostolic sent ones. Therefore, when they went forth in prayer and praise, it affected the atmosphere such that a great earthquake occurred and the foundations of the prison were shaken. These signs were a spiritual shifting taking place and naturally manifesting itself within the prison. This was because God was bringing judgment for them being imprisoned while making it clear that He had all dominion. Paul and Silas's prayer and praise also delivered the people that were bound in prison. The word says that the prison doors opened and the bands where loosed. God had changed their position in the spirit realm, and it manifested by the doors of their natural prisons being opened and them being freed from bondage. The reaction of such a move of God brought fear to the point of considering suicide rather than facing God. Yet God's desire is always initially to save so Paul let the guard know all was well. Thus, the guard and his entire household was saved and baptized.

The meaning of apostle translated in Latin is "*missio*," which means missionary. The apostle tends to operate as they are sent by God and are given strategic missions from him to advance his kingdom. Supernatural power, miracles, signs, and wonders are a trademark of their ministry.

> *Acts 5:12 Amplified Bible At the hands of the apostles many signs and wonders (attesting miracles) were continually taking place among the people. And by common consent they all met together [at the temple] in [the covered porch called] Solomon's portico.*

*Acts 19:11-17 The Amplified Bible God was doing extraordinary and unusual miracles by the hands of Paul, so that even handkerchiefs or face-towels or aprons that had touched his skin were brought to the sick, and their diseases left them and the evil spirits came out [of them].*

God was doing extraordinary miracles through the Apostle Paul that even cloth materials that he touched brought healing and deliverance to those who came in contact with them. Apostles should carry the power to bring forth healing, miracles, signs, and wonders, within their very nature.

*Luke 9:1-3 The Amplified Bible Then Jesus called together the Twelve [apostles] and gave them power and authority over all demons, and to cure diseases, And He sent them out to announce and preach the kingdom of God and bring healing. And He said to them, Do not take anything for your journey- neither walking stick, nor wallet [for a collection bag], nor food of any kind, nor money, and do not have two undergarment (tunics).*

Jesus bestowed the twelve apostles with power and authority over demons and the power to cure diseases. He sent them out on a mission to bring healing and preach the kingdom of God contesting against the demonic. He told them not to take anything with them, not food, wallets, money, or clothes to take care of themselves. As they were sent by God, they were also being supported and sustained in their assignment by God alone. Apostles must lean and trust solely in God to provide for their ministry. He will give them the strategy, supernatural provision, revelation, insight, and power they need to be fruitful in their assignments.

*1Corinthians 2:4-5 The Amplified Bible And my message and my preaching were not in persuasive words of wisdom [using clever rhetoric], but [they were delivered] in demonstration of the [Holy] Spirit [operating through me] and of [His] power [stirring the minds of the listeners and persuading them], so that your faith would not rest on the wisdom and rhetoric of men, but on the power of God.*

The ministry of the apostle is not found in intellectually clever rhetoric. It comes from the provision of God and exudes from the demonstration of the Holy Spirit and power that functions through them. The apostle is inclined to have direct insight, plans, and blueprints from God that map out what their purpose is each time they have a ministry assignment. They are typically agitated, frustrated, and sometimes lost if they are in an environment that has no direction, guidance, and purpose as it pertains to effective kingdom ministry. They can also be righteously angered if they are involved in ministry that has a self-agenda and is not God-focused or rooted in the fulfilling of his will, because this is the infrastructure and rock of their ministry. For them, everything is about what God is saying, doing, and willing to do. In the Amplified Version of *John 22:42*, Jesus says, *"not my will, but yours [always] be done."* This is how the apostle feels and how they live. Their purpose is to establish and fulfill the will of God in the earth realm.

> ***Titus 1:1-3 New Living Bible*** *This letter is from Paul, a slave of God and an apostle of Jesus Christ. I have been sent to proclaim faith to those God has chosen and to teach them to know the truth that shows them how to live godly lives. This truth gives them confidence that they have eternal life, which God – who does not lie – promised them before the world began. And now at just the right time he has revealed this message, which we announce to everyone. It is by the command of God our Savior that I have been entrusted with this work for him.*

Paul, an apostle of Jesus Christ, explains that as an apostle he had been sent and entrusted to proclaim the truth of God, such that people would be transformed into embodying God's holy and pure nature in their daily lives. The truth that he proclaimed drew people out of darkness and deception into the kingdom of God, trusting in the eternal life that Jesus provided for them. The apostle will release the truth of the kingdom of God through their ministry and destroy demonic deceptions that would block the people from being established in the kingdom. They carry a strong warfare capacity because they are called to overthrow demonic kingdoms and institute the kingdom of God in lives, regions, and entire territories. God's anointing upon the apostle causes them to combat, boldly confront, and demolish that which is not of God while bringing in what is of him, and what he may be specifically desiring to plant within a certain region and community of people. Since the apostles' ministry has a heavy dimension of warfare, they have been endowed with a unique power and authority that is distinct to their office, which aids them in successfully executing their God-ordained assignments.

> ***Luke 10:19 Amplified Bible*** *Listen carefully: I have given you authority [that you now possess] to tread on serpents and scorpions, and [the ability to exercise authority] over all the power of the enemy (Satan); and nothing will [in any way] harm you.*

> *Acts 19:1-9 Amplified Bible It happened that while Apollos was in Corinth, Paul went through the upper [inland] districts and came down to Ephesus, and found some disciples. He asked them, "Did you receive the Holy Spirit when you believed [in Jesus as the Christ]?" And they said, "No, we have not even heard that there is a Holy Spirit." And he asked, "Into what then were you baptized?" They said, "Into John's baptism." Paul said, "John performed a baptism of repentance, continually telling the people to believe in Him who was coming after him, that is, [to confidently accept and joyfully believe] in Jesus [the Messiah and Savior]." After hearing this, they were baptized [again, this time] in the name of the Lord Jesus. And when Paul laid his hands on them, the Holy Spirit came on them, and they began speaking in [unknown] tongues (languages) and prophesying. There were about twelve men in all.*
>
> *And he went into the synagogue and for three months spoke boldly, reasoning and arguing and persuading them about the kingdom of God. But when some were becoming hardened and disobedient [to the word of God], discrediting and speaking evil of the Way (Jesus, Christianity) before the congregation, Paul left them, taking the disciples with him, and went on holding daily discussions in the lecture hall of Tyrannus [instead of in the synagogue].*

Paul entered Ephesus, and there he met some believers. He asked them if they had received the Holy Spirit and when they said "*no*," he gave them knowledge that although the baptism of John was good, they also needed the baptism of the Holy Spirit. He baptized them, and immediately they began to speak in other tongues and prophesy. He elevated and SHIFTED them into a new dimension of God that had not yet been planted within their region. In **Romans 15:20**, Paul says, *"Accordingly I set a goal to preach the gospel, not where Christ's name was already known, so that I would not build on another man's foundation;"* Apostles are groundwork pioneers who build the foundation of the new revelation, insight, and knowledge that God gives them. They dig up and throw out the demonic while building the kingdom of God where the demonic once claimed rulership.

As Paul ministered in the synagogue of Ephesus, some became hard and disobedient to the word, and they discredited and spoke evil of what he has preaching. He was enduring warfare as he pioneered within the region. The devil was not happy that his demonic structures were tumbling down as the kingdom of God was being proclaimed. As the apostle pioneers, they may experience demonic resistance from people and demonic spirits that seek to hinder their work. But God will cover, protect, and give them the means to continue prospering in their mission. Paul left taking some of the disciples with him and held daily discussions in a lecture hall. The gospel and his purpose did not cease to flourish.

> ***Galatians 4:19 Amplified Bible*** *My little children, for whom I am again in [the pains of] labor until Christ is [completely and permanently] formed within you –*

The apostle will toil until Christ is formed. Their targeted intention is to see Jesus completely permeate the people and region eternally. Their ministry labors until the fullness of Christ has been birthed out and is in operation. When this happens, they slip to the side as Jesus and the Holy Spirit increases and takes over.

I would contend that a few scriptures are everyday truths for apostles:

> ***Joshua 1:3*** *Every place that the sole of your foot shall tread upon, that have I given unto you, as I said unto Moses.*

> ***Psalms 108:13*** *Through God we shall do valiantly: for he it is that shall tread down our enemies.*

> ***Matthew 10:8*** *Heal the sick, cleanse the lepers, raise the dead, cast out devils: freely ye have received, freely give.*

> ***Luke 10:19*** *Behold, I give unto you power to tread on serpents and scorpions, and overall the power of the enemy: and nothing shall by any means hurt you.*

> ***Acts 5:12*** *And by the hands of the apostles were many signs and wonders wrought among the people; (and they were all with one accord in Solomon's porch.*

Apostles have an appetite and a drive not to share space with wickedness. They find it difficult to hang out or minister in a service where there is mixture and where people are blind to the demonic workings occurring in their midst. They find it difficult to see people bound and remain silent while acting like God is getting glory, when his glory comes from people being saved and set free. Many apostles find this difficult at home, in the community, in their town - region, on their jobs, etc. Their very presentation and the fact that they simply walked onto - treaded upon a land - entered an atmosphere - creates a stirring that enrages demons. The apostle is also stirred by the righteous justice brooding within them. They are compelled to produce the kingdom of God at the expense of persecution and death. As to an apostle, the kingdom of God is always at hand, and it is their lifestyle to reveal God, declare God, establish God, by any means necessary.

> *Romans 8:36* As it is written, For thy sake we are killed all the day long; we are accounted as sheep for the slaughter.
>
> *Philippians 3:7-8* But whatever was an asset to me, I count as loss for the sake of Christ. More than that, I count all things as loss compared to the surpassing excellence of knowing Christ Jesus my Lord, for whom I have lost all things. I consider them rubbish, that I may gain Christ.
>
> *Matthew 11:12* And from the days of John the Baptist until now the kingdom of heaven suffereth violence, and the violent take it by force.
>
> *Mark 1:5* And saying, The time is fulfilled, and the kingdom of God is at hand: repent ye, and believe the gospel.
>
> *Luke 11:20* But if I with the finger of God cast out devils, no doubt the kingdom of God is come upon you.

Here is some insight into the mind of an apostle. They spend much time:

- ✓ Discerning what principalities are at work, what strongholds are in the region and in the people, and what weapons need to be used to overthrow the enemy.
- ✓ Discerning SHIFTS in the spirit realm where an opportune time is being presented to annihilate strongholds and displace principalities.
- ✓ Discerning whether God even wants to work as though we recognize a need for deliverance and breakthrough, the people of that region must be ready to sustain what God does; otherwise the enemy will return with a vengeance and stronghold them worse than before.

> *Ephesians 6:12-13* For we wrestle not against flesh and blood, but against principalities, against powers, against the rulers of the darkness of this world, against spiritual wickedness in high places. Wherefore take unto you the whole armour of God, that ye may be able to withstand in the evil day, and having done all, to stand.

Because of the armored mantle of God is upon the apostle, they are either loved or hated. They are misunderstood or accepted for their peculiarity. They are received or dreadfully rejected. The mantle upon them demands holiness and the excellency of God. You probably have heard it called "apostolic order." Apostles are ordained to bring the alignment of God to anything that is misaligned. It is an innate quality and aura radiating from them. They are not trying to judge disorder and unholiness; the God in them automatically judges disorder and unholiness. Therefore, when they walk in a room, even before they do anything, judgment begins. Many people are intimidated by this. Many will often shun or avoid the apostle because they feel threatened by what is automatically bringing awareness and conviction to the misalignment that is within them. Apostles usually must approach people and demonstrate the love and compassion of God, so that people will relax and embrace the fullness of who they are, and not reject them because of the godly mantle that is upon them that they have no control over. Apostles must be okay that this is a part of their identity and influence or insecurity will cause them to abuse their authority where they come across as critical and emotionally judgmental, as opposed to operating through the confidence of healthy discernment and divine justice.

An apostle pioneering a ministry that is still being embraced in the body of Christ can find themselves enduring continual persecution. Not being content in one's identity can increase the warfare as the enemy will use the ignorance and religious mindsets of people to distract, dismantle, and disempower the work and vision God has granted to the apostle's hands. An insecure, broken or confused identity will have the apostle wavering, doubting God, angry and resentful, as they strive to do what God says do, and navigate through the treasons of those the apostle will minister and impart into. God will require the apostle to have grace and compassion for them regardless of how they reject, neglect, and dishonor the apostle. Please understand that this is a part of one's journey as an apostle and that their actions will hurt. Despite what the apostle will endure, the person will have to still give them all God is requiring through the apostolic calling that is upon their life. A healthy identity will allow the apostle to remain focused and grounded as they trail blaze, plant, plow, and build for God's glory.

Apostles need to know their authority so they can tower over the demonic forces that will contend against them. When apostles do not know their authority, demonic forces and religious people use this as an opportunity to snuff out the work of God. Their ministry can be a blessing, but they lack the power and definition to bring the full will of God to pass. People will also find it difficult to grasp what the apostle is ministering because if the apostle is not clear regarding their authority, then neither will others be clear regarding it. Often, our wells are revealed through the dimension of ministry that manifest the strongest in our lives. Usually, God teaches the dimensions of ministry first, then over time, he reveals the mantle of apostleship. The person will sometimes be used in various other office positions such as prophet, teacher, evangelist, pastor, before they realize they are an apostle. The person's authority is being solidified and is increasing during these seasons, as they learn the value and operation of the other offices and how they work with and empower the apostle. If the apostle is insecure in these seasons, it will be interwoven in their identity as an apostle. In order to operate in true apostolic authority, the apostle must first be healed in their identity. Healing will purify the apostle's identity and bring clarity to their well of apostolic authority.

As an apostle grows in their calling, they will be able to identify with other apostles. However, it will take a daily walk with God to unveil the full vision and pattern of who they are in the earth. There will be parts of the apostle's calling that are strategic to who they are, and they will not find a pattern of it in the earth. A relationship with the Holy Spirit will enable the apostle to maneuver efficiently and successfully through seasons of uncertainty, persecution, and development. This will be key in growing in the precision, grace, and authority in the fullness of one's apostolic calling. As the person grows as an apostle, they will be more effective and demonstrative with miracles, signs, and wonders following.

## PROPHETS OFFICE

> *2Kings 17:13 New Living Bible Again and again the Lord had sent his prophets and seers to warn both Israel and Judah: "Turn from all your evil ways. Obey my commands and decrees – the entire law that I commanded your ancestors to obey, and that I gave you through my servants the prophets."*

<u>Prophets</u> in the Strong's Concordance means:
1. Inspired man
2. Spokesman

3. Speaker

<u>Seer</u> in the Strong's Concordance means:
1. A beholder in vision
2. Stargazer
3. Prophet
4. Vision

> ***Deuteronomy 18:18 English Standard Bible*** *I will raise up for them a prophet like you from among their brothers. And I will put my words in his mouth, and he shall speak to them all that I command him.*

Prophets are inspired spokesman and visionaries of God who release the words, commands, and standards of the Lord in the earth. Whether the people or regions receive, align, and grasp the revelation being released, the prophet must fearlessly proclaim what God is showing or speaking to them (*Exodus 4:12*). God puts his word in the prophet and through their bodies and very existence, they release what is on the heart and mind of God for the people, regions, and territories they minister to. True prophets know that it is key for them to be connected to God such that they can minister from a place of revelation and conveyed knowledge. They are inspired by what is seen and heard from God within the realm of the spirit. They operate from what they see God doing, hear God doing, and bring what they experience in the spirit into natural manifestation. They desire to provoke a turning and surrendering to the laws and decrees of God.

> ***Revelation 1:10-11 New American Bible*** *I was caught up in spirit on the Lord's day and heard behind me a voice as loud as a trumpet, which said, "Write on a scroll what you see and send it to the seven churches: to Ephesus, Smyrna, Pergamum, Thyatira, Sardis, Philadelphia, and Laodicea."*

Often times, they are caught up in the spirit as God speaks to them and gives them vision concerning what they are to minister. It is one thing for a prophet to have the ability to ascend into the heavenly places at any moment, but it is a whole other thing for that minister to be able to translate what they see, hear, and experience in heaven into the earth. This is a key to being an effective prophet. They must be able to bring heaven to earth or a dimension of their ministry will be missing. Their heavenly visitations will be a blessing to them, but not minister to others. As they know how to effectively operate in their calling, they have the power to write upon the people, atmosphere, and region through their prophetic words, utterances, visions, and dreams.

The prophet officer is first a watchman, intercessor, and lived a life communed with God. As the prophetic officer is continuously seeking the Lord and his spiritual realms, so they do not miss what God is doing and saying, and as a result, cause others to miss out as well. *Amos 3:7 New Living Bible* says, "*Indeed, the Sovereign Lord never does anything until he reveals his plans to his servants the prophets.*" God has secret counsel and conversation with his prophets, which is why it is important for them to stay in tune with God and His spirit. Since only God could communicate these secrets to them, they bring healing and deliverance to people's lives.

People are blessed by the prophet, but can sometimes be taken aback or resistant because they know things only God would know. They utilize their sight in the spirit realm and revealed secrets from God to minister immense transformation to all who receive of them.

> *Jeremiah 7:21-28 English Standard Bible Thus says the Lord of hosts, the God of Israel: "Add your burnt offerings to your sacrifices, and eat the flesh. For in the day that I brought them out of the land of Egypt, I did not speak to your fathers or command them concerning burnt offerings and sacrifices. But this command I gave them: 'Obey my voice, and I will be your God, and you shall be my people. And walk in all the way that I command you, that it may be well with you.' But they did not obey or incline their ear, but walked in their own counsels and the stubbornness of their evil hearts, and went backward and not forward.*
>
> *From the day that your fathers came out of the land of Egypt to this day, I have persistently sent all my servants the prophets to them, day after day. Yet they did not listen to me or incline their ear, but stiffened their neck. They did worse than their fathers. "So you shall speak all these words to them, but they will not listen to you. You shall call to them, but they will not answer you. And you shall say to them, 'This is the nation that did not obey the voice of the Lord their God, and did not accept discipline; truth has perished; it is cut off from their lips.*
>
> ***Acts 7:52 English Standard Bible*** *Which of the prophets did your fathers not persecute? And they killed those who announced beforehand the coming of the Righteous One, whom you have now betrayed and murdered.*

They encounter warfare from people and regions because the word they embody demands a surrendering and aligning to the commands of God. They command change, which causes them to press against those who are not willing to change, and demonic powers that have locked regions and people, thus inhibiting them from change.

- Prophetic officers do not just *nabi*. *Nabi* is Hebrew word *"to bubble forth, as from a fountain, hence to utter,"* generally when by Holy Spirit unction, when the glory of God is strong in the atmosphere or the spirit of prophecy is present (***Psalms 145:1, 1Samuel 9:9***).
- Though operable prophetic officers do not just give spontaneous prophetic words (***1Chronicles 25:1, 1Samuel 10:5, 2Kings 3:14–16). Ephesians 5:18–19***)
- Prophetic officers to not just encourage, edify, or exhort by operating through the gift of prophecy (***1Corinthians 14:3***).

Prophetic officers do not just create through words revealed by the presence of the Holy Spirit (***2Peter 1:19-21***). They may, however, utilize Holy Spirit words to create and cultivate people, atmospheres, and regions, while commanding them to manifest, commanding heaven to earth, or those who received them place a demand on them manifests. Holy Spirit words have more freewill, grace and compassion. They guide people into truth and can be processed out in relations to what people can handle, where they are and where they need to be in God. Such words also possess the feelings, emotions, heart, and compassion of God. Prophetic officers may release such prophecies, but these can also be released by the average saint and those with the gift of prophecy.

Those in office have prophetic authorities beyond these realms which distinguish them from those who desire to prophecy. Prophetic officers are the voice of heaven and their words carry the government weight of heaven.

The words of a prophetic officer are the reality of heaven, the potential of earth and are birthed through the glory and presence of God. Jesus denotes the literal office of a defined prophet because of his seat at the right hand of God. Prophets govern through their prophetic seat as an officer and legislate through the essence of Jesus. Having the ear and voice of Jesus is what separates the prophet from being prophetic and operating through the gift of prophecy, to delivering through the seated prophet's office. Jesus' words through the prophet asserts justice, judgment, righteousness as they charge, rebuke, correct, convict, warn, decree, and govern.  They assert the promises, vows, laws, purposes, and standards of heaven, particularly the right side of the throne room of God where Jesus sits.  Their words are matter of fact, defy and overrule man and demons, and are birthed and spoken through resurrection power.  They judge and nullify death while producing eternal life and kingdom judgment through whatever is spoken.

There is a righteous indignation and a righteous anger that manifests when speaking the prophecies given through the voice of Jesus.  There is a tendency to be moved by compassion, but this is because of the Holy Spirit coming upon the prophet, yet Jesus words are factual, finite, and alarming.  Jesus fulfills and sets the record straight, and so will the prophet when he or she is operating through the authority of his prophetic utterances.

> **Romans 8:34** *Who is he that condemneth? It is Christ that died, yea rather, that is risen again, who is even at the right hand of God, who also maketh intercession for us."*

*Right hand* is a place of honor and authority; it is a position of justice, judgment, and power.  The gavel of justice is hit with the right hand.  Swearings, laws, and verdicts are released with the gavel of the right hand.  Jesus is seated on the right as he completes and fulfills the law.  The prophet encounters him, hears, and asserts the justice and rulership that he has fulfilled in the earth.

> **Ephesians 1:20-22** *Which he wrought in Christ, when he raised him from the dead, and set him at his own right hand in the heavenly places," Far above all principality, and power, and might, and dominion, and every name that is named, not only in this world, but also in that which is to come: And hath put all things under his feet, and gave him to be the head over all things to the church, Which is his body, the fullness of him that filleth all in all.*

*Set* denotes established authority, rulership, and judgment.  Jesus is the name above every name, so his words carry a level of authority that everyone has to adhere and bow to.  His words are without negotiation as he is the only one who can change them.  When the prophet prophecies through the voice of Jesus,  they are releasing a word that defies everyone and everything.  This posture of a prophetic authority judges, and asserts dominion over principalities and powers, while placing everything under the feet - the jurisdiction of Jesus.

> ***Colossians 3:1*** *If ye then be risen with Christ, seek those things which are above, where Christ sitteth on the right hand of God.*

Prophets that hear through the well of Jesus learn to live in the heavenly places with him. They seek to hear, abide, and operate from this position as it is one of honor and authority in who they are in Jesus and who he is in him.

> ***Hebrews 1:3, 13*** *Who being the brightness of his glory, and the express image of his person, and upholding all things by the word of his power, when he had by himself purged our sins, sat down on the right hand of the Majesty on high . . . But to which of the angels said he at any time, Sit on my right hand, until I make thine enemies thy footstool?*

Jesus came to overthrow the enemy. This is his mandate even in his resurrection. His resurrection is proof that the enemy is his footstool. Prophets release this clarity and truth in the earth as they prophecy through the jurisdiction and resurrection power of Jesus.

> ***Hebrews 8:1*** *Now of the things which we have spoken this is the sum: We have such an high priest, who is set on the right hand of the throne of the Majesty in the heavens.*

> *Sum* in Greek is *kephalaion* and means, *"a principal thing, i.e. main point; specially, an amount (of money)."*

It is that which is important, essential, or the main point of a matter. This also denotes keys and strategies as what is spoken unlocks and releases what is necessary to bring Jesus' word and justice forth.

> ***Hebrew 8:1 The Message Bible*** *In essence, we have just such a high priest: authoritative right alongside God, conducting worship in the one true sanctuary built by God.*

> ***Hebrews 10:12*** *But this man, after he had offered one sacrifice for sins for ever, sat down on the right hand of God.*

Jesus eternally annihilated sin and death and took his seat. He did this with literal life. Imagine communing and receiving prophetic words and even reflecting and representing an office that has conquered sin and death. This is the truth - the reality as one who walks in the office of a prophet. The prophet carries the mantle to judge and overthrow sin and death. The words that come from the prophet carries resurrection power that sets order of the perfected will of God in the earth. Jesus restored the earth.

> ***Hebrews 12:2*** *Looking unto Jesus the author and finisher of our faith; who for the joy that was set before him endured the cross, despising the shame, and is set down at the right hand of the throne of God.*

Prophets should complete whatever they start. Their office requires that. They are the gavel that seals Jesus's work in the earth.

> ***1Peter 3:22*** *Who is gone into heaven, and is on the right hand of God; angels and authorities and powers being made subject unto him.*

<u>Subject</u> in Greek is *hypotassō* and means: fix this space

1. to subordinate; reflexively, to obey, to be under obedience (obedient), put under
2. subdue unto, (be, make) subject (to, unto), be (put) in subjection (to, under), submit self unto
3. to arrange under, to subordinate to subject, put in subjection to, subject one's self, obey
4. to submit to one's control
5. to yield to one's admonition or advice, to obey, be subject
6. A Greek military term meaning "to arrange [troop divisions] in a military fashion under the command of a leader."
7. In non-military use, it was "a voluntary attitude of giving in, cooperating, assuming responsibility, and carrying a burden."

This is the level of authority and power an officer walks in as a prophet. The officer is subjecting everything to the footstool of Jesus. There is no negotiation, free will, or compromise. Even if people do not want to adhere to the word they are subject to Jesus in the prophet. They must bow anyway or risk judgment. God set up that way. When the prophetic officer understands this level of their mantle and begin to walk in it, they can release justice and judgment through the dominion of what Jesus did on the cross, as it no longer becomes about what people are willing to receive, but what Jesus already did, it is finished, so it requires no proving or action. Everything has already been destined to be subjected to what he did. The prophetic officer is simply legislating that finite truth in the earth.

> ***1Peter 3:22 The Message Bible*** *Jesus has the last word on everything and everyone, from angels to armies. He's standing right alongside God, and what he says goes.*

Prophetic officers are **authorized by God** to warn, correct, and caution people, ministries and regions. God may also unction a prophet to minister judgment to people, demons, and regions if there has been no repentance regarding his previous warnings and commands. The warnings, corrections, cautions and judgments prophets release **are God inspired – God directed – God led**. Their purpose to restore and realign people back to God, as the seat of Jesus is one of salvation and eternal life, so prophets should legislate warnings and judgment from this heart posture and mind set.

> ***2Peter 1:21 English Standard Bible*** *For no prophecy was ever produced by the will of man, but men spoke from God as they were carried along by the Holy Spirit.*

> ***Jeremiah 1:9 English Standard Bible*** *Then the Lord put out his hand and touched my mouth. And the Lord said to me, "Behold, I have put my words in your mouth.*

---

*The warnings, corrections, cautions and judgments prophets release are God inspired – God directed – God led*

---

This is important to note because many prophets can succumb to error, emotions, or witchcraft, by using their position of authority as an officer to release words of warning, correction, caution, and judgment to punish, control, manipulate others. They may do this because they believe it is right in their own eyes or for influence and advancement.

When God release these kinds words, he is sharing truth of the consequences of sin actions. However, such prophetic words are not initially to condemn people to damnation or to hell, but to restore them, as God is first about restoration. Jesus was constantly insighting repentance and even judgement for the purpose of saving lives. *"Repent, for the kingdom of heaven is at hand"* was the motto of his life (***Matthew 3:2***). The entire reason Jesus came was to restore us in eternal life with God. The prophet is given the authority of these words because they speak through the posture of Jesus who is justice, judgement, restoration, and salvation. Therefore, when these words are given, they should be for the purposes of restoring people, ministries, regions, in salvation with God. If we also consider the biblical prophets of the Old Testament, we can discern that every prophetic warning, judgement, etc., accompanied with God's desire to see them restored through repentance and relationship unto him. The warnings, cautions, and judgments are what could happen if they do not align or realign. When the prophet is wanting judgement over restoration, they have usurped their authority as a prophet and have become idolatrous, demonic, and/or self-absorbed in their office as a prophet. Jonah had such a posture that resulted in a fish swallow him.

When studying to book of Jonah, we find God giving Jonah assignment to go cry aloud against the wickedness of the people of Nineveh. But Jonah paid a fare to flee to Tarnish by way of a ship because he did not want to give the word. His reasoning was that he knew that if they repent, God would deliver them. Jonah was on the ship sleeping while the men were seeking God for the purpose of the tumultuous judging winds that seemed to roar as they were sailing to Tarnish. The shipmaster woke Jonah up and demanded he cry out to God with them. After casting lots and Jonah confessing, it was revealed that the evil winds were due to him running from God. They had no choice but to throw him overboard to get the evil winds to cease. Once overboard a fish swallowed Jonah. He was inside the fish three days and three nights. Jonah reluctantly humbled himself while inside the fish. God spared him, the fish vomited Jonah on dry land, and God required him again to go deliver his word to Nineveh.

In Jonah chapter 3, Jonah preached warnings and judgment against Nineveh for forty days. This lets us know that Nineveh did not immediately take heed to what Jonah was proclaiming against them. However, they were eventually pricked to conviction by Jonah's outcry, and sought God with fasting and repentance. God accepted their fast and repentance and withdrew his judgment.

> ***Verse 5-10*** *So the people of Nineveh believed God, and proclaimed a fast, and put on sackcloth, from the greatest of them even to the least of them. For word came unto the king of Nineveh, and he arose from his throne,*

*and he laid his robe from him, and covered him with sackcloth, and sat in ashes. And he caused it to be proclaimed and published through Nineveh by the decree of the king and his nobles, saying, Let neither man nor beast, herd nor flock, taste any thing: let them not feed, nor drink water: But let man and beast be covered with sackcloth, and cry mightily unto God: yea, let them turn every one from his evil way, and from the violence that is in their hands. Who can tell if God will turn and repent, and turn away from his fierce anger, that we perish not? And God saw their works, that they turned from their evil way; and God repented of the evil, that he had said that he would do unto them; and he did it not.*

Jonah was displeased by God's forgiveness. He was so grieved by it and thus wanted to die. He told God that the reason he fled from proclaiming the word was because he knew God would forgive them and withdraw his judgement.

***Jonah 4:1-3*** *But it displeased Jonah exceedingly, and he was very angry. And he prayed unto the Lord, and said, I pray thee, O Lord, was not this my saying, when I was yet in my country? Therefore I fled before unto Tarshish: for I knew that thou art a gracious God, and merciful, slow to anger, and of great kindness, and repentest thee of the evil. Therefore now, O Lord, take, I beseech thee, my life from me; for it is better for me to die than to live.*

What a horrible posture for a saint but especially a mouthpiece of God. Fleeing so he would not have to give a word that would turn a people back to God, then being grieved unto death that restoration occurred. As Jonah grieved, God took him through a trial to show him that his posture as a prophet was ungodly. Even in that trial, Jonah was self-absorbed and asked God to kill him so he did not have to endure the trial. He was not able to recognize that God was using the situation to prove a point of how repentance and restoration rather than death and destruction, was his ultimate desire with his people.

***Verse 4-11*** *Then said the Lord, Doest thou well to be angry? So Jonah went out of the city, and sat on the east side of the city, and there made him a booth, and sat under it in the shadow, till he might see what would become of the city. And the Lord God prepared a gourd, and made it to come up over Jonah, that it might be a shadow over his head, to deliver him from his grief. So Jonah was exceeding glad of the gourd. But God prepared a worm when the morning rose the next day, and it smote the gourd that it withered. And it came to pass, when the sun did arise, that*

> *God prepared a vehement east wind; and the sun beat upon the head of Jonah, that he fainted, and wished in himself to die, and said, It is better for me to die than to live. And God said to Jonah, Doest thou well to be angry for the gourd? And he said, I do well to be angry, even unto death. Then said the Lord, Thou hast had pity on the gourd, for the which thou hast not laboured, neither madest it grow; which came up in a night, and perished in a night: And should not I spare Nineveh, that great city, wherein are more than sixscore thousand persons that cannot discern between their right hand and their left hand; and also much cattle?*

Prophets with Jonah's disposition are dangerous. They have the gift, office, and authority of God but not the character, nature, and heart of God.

- They would rather see people judged, suffering, and destroyed than restored in right fellowship with God.
- They are vexed when God forgives because they want to see the warnings and judgments come to pass.
- They usurp God by striving to punish the people for their sins rather than allowing the word to be the punishment needed to drive people to repentance and right fellowship with God.
- They either do not discern or dread that God's prophecies, even his warnings, cautions, corrections, and judgments, are not about harming people, but about provoking people to deliverance.

Such prophets will go to great lengths to have their judgments manifests, even to the extent of refusing to give warnings; even to the extent of risking their own relationships and lives being destroyed. This is not God's disposition of a prophet. God's prophet has his heart. God so loved the world that he gave his only begotten son that it should not perish but have everlasting life (*John 3:16*). This is the heart of a prophet – that he or she would sacrifice their own lives so that others might be saved. Jesus just wanted to please God. This was his meat and his will, even at the expense of his own life.

> *John 4:34 Jesus saith unto them, My meat is to do the will of him that sent me, and to finish his work.*

Another way heartless prophets operate, is by giving warnings, cautions, corrections, and judgments that God did not release. It will be for the purposes of getting people to repent for matters the prophet believes the people should turn from or should do. Often such words are given by an immature or wounded prophet officer who has not been taught how to properly govern in the office of a prophet and who is not grounded in the character and nature of the Lord. Though not always the case,

- They may contend they are called to warn and judge.
- They may be adamant that this is their calling, while lacking understanding and balance in the full official duties of a prophet.
- Their prophets' blessings and exhortations are usually soulish, conditional, and self-serving. They are to draw people to them and ensue favor with people than to draw them to God. The minute a person does something they do not like, they become offended, or their word is rejected, they withdraw their blessings and exhortations and release false warnings and damnations.

Some of these prophets will engage in religious acts of fasting, consecrating, and continuously praying, while contending they are interceding for the people to receive their word so they can turn from what they perceived to be "their wicked ways." But truly they are operating through a religious spirit that has them engaging in religious rectory that appear to be godly, but has now become witchcraft, because their motive is about seducing and manipulating the spirit realm to get people to do what they want them to do. This is no different than witches who fast, consecrate and chant witchcraft spells and curses to impact and manipulate the lives of people. Such prophets only care about seeing their word coming to pass so they can validate their prophetic office and their self-righteous stance. For those who have been rejected or whose word has been rejected, their mandate is proving they heard from God and that they are a prophet of God.

- They do not discern that the words they heard are from the wounds of their souls and are possibly demonic, because they have postured their ear to emotions, the second heaven, and even to the gateway of demons.
- Like Jonah, these erred prophets are prideful, self-righteous, and unrepentant. They will not admit the error of their ways and therefore, tend to destroy lives with their manipulative religious acts, rather than save them.
- Because they are adamant that they are carrying the judgments of the Lord, it will be difficult for them to receive truth and be delivered. Remember Jonah rather died than to admit he was out of order, and that restoration was the honorable way of the Lord.

> *Jeremiah 9:23-24* Thus saith the Lord, Let not the wise man glory in his wisdom, neither let the mighty man glory in his might, let not the rich man glory in his riches: But let him that glorieth glory in this, that he understandeth and knoweth me, that I am the Lord which exercise lovingkindness, judgment, and righteousness, in the earth: for in these things I delight, saith the Lord.

Prophets should never abuse their positions of authority. Just because they are the mouthpiece of God, does not give them the right to lord over people, demand their words to be received, or cast judgment without God's permission. When a prophet SHIFTS beyond God's scope of delivering a word, they are in error and are operating in witchcraft.

> *Jeremiah 14:14* The prophets are prophesying lies in My name," the LORD replied. "I did not send them or appoint them or speak to them. They are prophesying to you a false vision, a worthless divination, the futility and delusion of their own minds.

> *Ezekiel 13:3-6* Thus saith the Lord God; Woe unto the foolish prophets, that follow their own spirit, and have seen nothing! O Israel, thy prophets are like the foxes in the deserts. Ye have not gone up into the gaps, neither made up the hedge for the house of Israel to stand in the battle in the day of the Lord. They have seen vanity and lying divination, saying, The Lord saith: and the Lord hath not sent them: and they have made others to hope that they would confirm the word.

It is not that you are no longer a prophet, you are now a lying prophet operating as a witch. You have become an enemy of the Lord rather than a mouthpiece of the Lord. You have the same power and authority but it is now used for evil rather than good. In *2Chronicles 18* a prophet was hated by a king for only speaking what God said - no more and no less.

> *Verse 7* And the king of Israel said unto Jehoshaphat, There is yet one man, by whom we may enquire of the Lord: but I hate him; for he never prophesied good unto me, but always evil: the same is Micaiah the son of Imla. And Jehoshaphat said, Let not the king say so.

> *Verse 12-17* And the messenger that went to call Micaiah spake to him, saying, Behold, the words of the prophets declare good to the king with one assent; let thy word therefore, I pray thee, be like one of theirs, and speak thou good. And Micaiah said, As the Lord liveth, even what my God saith, that will I speak. And when he was come to the king, the king said unto him, Micaiah, shall we go to Ramothgilead to battle, or shall I

*forbear? And he said, Go ye up, and prosper, and they shall be delivered into your hand. And the king said to him, How many times shall I adjure thee that thou say nothing but the truth to me in the name of the Lord? Then he said, I did see all Israel scattered upon the mountains, as sheep that have no shepherd: and the Lord said, These have no master; let them return therefore every man to his house in peace. And the king of Israel said to Jehoshaphat, Did I not tell thee that he would not prophesy good unto me, but evil?*

The king saw this as evil because the prophet never spoke anything he wanted to hear. The king only wanted prophetic words that aligned with his desires with no regard to the purposes of the Lord for his life, the people, and kingdom he was governing. His mindset about prophecy was twisted and erred. He lacked revelation that prophecy was about God's will being done in the earth and not for his personal pleasure and gain. This is a key that prophet officers must live by and serve through. Prophecy is for God's glory, God's purpose, God's covenant, eternal life with God, and God's kingdom being advanced in the earth. Prophets do not prophecy what people want to hear, but what God speaks. And regardless to whether people receive or reject the word, they do not SHIFT beyond God's scope of delivery. Therefore if God is not leading them to,

- Cry aloud - constantly warn the people
- Fast, consecrate and pray
- Release judgment
- Set siege as a sign unto the people (Study Jeremiah)
- Engage in bizarre signs and wonders (Study Ezekiel)

then they are out of order. They have done their job as prophet officers by releasing the word and moving on. I spent extensive time sharing this insight because it is vital to a prophet not overstepping boundaries in their prophetic office. We must restore the trust between prophets and people where we send for prophets rather than dread their presence. People need to feel safe with prophets. They need to know they can trust the prophet to guide them through the justice seat of Jesus. They need to know that prophets embody the heart of God and want God's will and purpose for their lives. I decree that a SHIFT is occurring where prophets are sought out because they possess divine integrity to SHIFT people, nations, and spheres through the prophetic word of God.

Another facet of the prophet's office is decreeing through the sovereignty of God. Apostles and prophets have this authority. Let's take a moment to clarify how the sovereignty of God's prophetic decrees manifests:

- ✓ God's words are sovereign, governmental, and manifest through the monarchy of heaven. They cannot be vetoed. They do not return void and are destined to come to pass.
- ✓ God's words reveal the end from the beginning. They are foundational and were here at the beginning of time as he created the heavens and the earth. They are being unveiled and completed as the prophet speaks them, but rarely are they new from God, new in heaven, new to the earth, even though they are new to people and evolving from the earth and heavenly spheres.
- ✓ When God is giving the prophet a word to release, they are revealing and conveying what has already been established and said before the beginning of time.

*Isaiah 46:10 Declaring the end from the beginning, and from ancient times the things that are not yet done, saying, My counsel shall stand, and I will do all my pleasure.*

Prophetic officers train others to hear God and properly release his word, pioneer and oversee schools of the prophets, scribe curriculum to equip the body of Christ in the gift and office of a prophet (***Study 1Samuel 19:18-24, 2Kings 2, 2Kings 4:38-44, 2Kings 9:1-3, 2Chronicles 18:5-19***)

## EVANGELIST OFFICE

Evangelist in Greek is *euangelos*. *Eu* means "*good*" and "*angelos*" nearly always translated as "angel."

Evangelist means "*messenger;*" "*one who is sent in order to announce, teach, or perform a thing.*"

- ✓ They proclaim a good message or good news.
- ✓ They preach and legislate the Gospel, enact good tidings, show glad tidings, as it pertains to the gospel.
- ✓ They SHIFT people into relationship with the message of salvation- which is Jesus Christ.

I would boast that evangelistic officers are confronting warring foot soldiers. They take the gospel directly to the people, lands, and, regions while confronting and overthrowing powers of darkness. Evangelist legislate by manifesting the authoritative message of Jesus and his saving drawing power.

*The weapons of an evangelist officer:*

- ❖ The coming of Jesus to earth
- ❖ The blood of Jesus
- ❖ The cross of Jesus
- ❖ The works of Jesus on through cross
- ❖ The resurrection power of Jesus

Evangelistic officers preach and legislate Jesus and Jesus crucified while demonstrating his saving power.

> ***1Corinthians 2:1-5*** *And I, brethren, when I came to you, came not with excellency of speech or of wisdom, declaring unto you the testimony of God. For I determined not to know anything among you, save Jesus Christ, and him crucified. And I was with you in weakness, and in fear, and in much trembling. And my speech and my preaching was not with enticing words of man's wisdom, but in demonstration of the Spirit and of power: That your faith should not stand in the wisdom of men, but in the power of God.*

Evangelistic officers embody the message of Jesus. They have a heart and mandate for the people to connect and come into right standing and relationship with Christ. Evangelist bring a message of conviction that draws people to Christ with hope and faith that God is the deliverer, healer, savior, and answer to their every situation. They enact good tidings, show glad tidings, and minister the gospel with boldness while releasing the love, joy, salvation, redemption, and message of Jesus Christ. Their ministry and office always ties back to Jesus, who he is to us, what he did for us, and what he has made available for us. Although there is great joy released through the ministry of the evangelist, it is not always about expressing the joy of the Lord. It will also display lowliness, brokenness, hurt, and woundedness, in order to relate to people's situations, cause them to be convicted to look at themselves and their current situations, and see why they need Jesus in their lives. Evangelist will easily show a depiction of the people, and the people will be able to connect because they feel like "oh, that's me." They will feel like the evangelist is telling their story because of how relatable it is and how the evangelist has interjected into their lives and situations. This interjection is key as those in the office literally becoming commanding governors by using the message they are imparting to dismantle sins and demonic influences. It is like Jesus taking their burdens and lifting things off of and up out of people, places, and things, as the evangelist ministers healing, deliverance, and cleansing, setting them free of their challenges.

> **1Peter 5:7** *Casting all your care upon him; for he careth for you.*

> **Psalms 55:22** *Cast thy burden upon the LORD, and he shall sustain thee: he shall never suffer the righteous to be moved.*

The evangelist always has desires for the people to be saved, come into the knowledge of Jesus, and the truth that he is the one and only God who has the power to save them. As an officer, the evangelist is constantly making sure souls are being saved. They pursue souls everywhere the souls of their feet tread and can pick up on the burdens of the people, land, and regions as they navigate territories and spheres.

> **1Timothy 2:4-5** *Who will have all men to be saved, and to come unto the knowledge of the truth. For there is one God, and one mediator between God and men, the man Christ Jesus.*

They often display and minister on how the power of Jesus, the gospel, and the message they are proclaiming brings transformation, healing, miracles, and deliverance into their lives, churches, communities, and regions.

> **Romans 1:16 New Living Bible** *For I am not ashamed of this Good News about Christ. It is the power of God at work, saving everyone who believes – the Jew first and also the Gentile.*

> **Joshua 1:3** *Every place that the sole of your foot shall tread upon, that have I given unto you, as I said unto Moses.*

> **Acts 1:8** *But ye shall receive power, after that the Holy Ghost is come upon you: and ye shall be witnesses unto me both in Jerusalem, and in all Judaea, and in Samaria, and unto the uttermost part of the earth.*

<u>Power</u> in the Strong's Concordance in this scripture means:
1. Force
2. Miraculous power, a miracle itself, ability, abundance
3. Power, strength, violence, mighty (wonderful) work

4. Inherit power, power residing in a thing by virtue of its nature, or which a person or thing exerts and puts forth power for performing miracles
5. Moral power and excellence of soul
6. The power and influence which belong to riches and wealth
7. Power and resources arising from numbers
8. Power consisting in or resisting in or resting upon armies, forces, hosts

The power for miracles, strength, influence, and heavenly resources is released through the message of Jesus that they carry.

Evangelism is a soul winning ministry. Therefore it goes to war with the darkness set against the souls of the people, lands, regions, and spheres. Often, we are taught that the evangelist ministry is about drawing people and bringing them to church. But there is war on this ministry because after drawing the people, the demonic bondages upon their souls must be dealt with to help them sustain in the Lord, and truly see their lives transformed. So evangelistic offices draw people, war for their souls, then command the government of God to overtake their souls such that pursue to live eternally for God.

In Greek literature, *evangelizo* was also used of liberation from enemies as well as deliverance from demonic power. As the evangelist goes forth, they deliver and liberate people from the bondages of sin and demonic powers that have claim over them. They transfer lives from the ownership of darkness into the ownership of light. They aim to gain dominion of souls for the kingdom of God.

> *1Peter 2:9 But ye are a chosen generation, a royal priesthood, an holy nation, a peculiar people; that ye should shew forth the praises of him who hath called you out of darkness into his marvellous light.*

Evangelistic officers also oversee and legislate evangelistic teams, mission's works, while equipping the body of Christ in outreach ministry. They are effective and creative in pioneering social service works, visions, and teams that infiltrate organizations, systems, communities, regions, nations, and save souls for God's glory. As part of their mandate is to mobilize the body of Christ to be a light and to position themselves to be a light for Christ. For an evangelistic officer, every moment is always a great opportunity to save a soul. Jesus in them is always looking to deliver, heal, and free the hurting and dying, so they will want to go where the lost are, even at the risk of their own lives. They will prefer hands on training as opposed to sitting in a room teaching and training on evangelism. Though this has its place, and they required to do it, they prefer and will demand hands on trench evangelistic training. They believe the best way to learn to save souls is to get out and do just that. Once pioneered, the evangelistic officer will place a leader over these particular works so that they can continue to avenues for salvation.

Many evangelistic officers possess a well of the prophetic. This is because the testimony of Jesus Christ is the spirit of prophecy (***Revelation 19:10***). They embody the salvation of Jesus and proclaim his workings, so this creates a lifestyle and atmosphere for prophecy to flow. The more they intertwine what they preach to the deliverance, healing, and salvation of Jesus, the greater the spirit of prophecy will work in and around them. They will be able to tape into the prophetic words of Jesus and speak into the lives and future of those they evangelize. Prophecy definitely strengthens the power of evangelism as it demonstrates a personal touch and encounter from Jesus himself. As people realize they are on the heart of Jesus and that Jesus cares about what concerns them, they are more likely to turn their lives over to him.

Most evangelistic officers prophecy from the compassion of Jesus. Some possess the authority to correct, rebuke, warn and expose. Such authorities should only be utilized at God's leading and for the purposes of drawing the soul to the saving power of Jesus.

### *Evangelistic Officer Qualities*

- ✓ Shares the good news of the gospel while seeking to save souls; focuses on the salvation of the person by introducing people to Christ, ministering the love of God for his people, and minister's salvation.
- ✓ Provokes change in the inner man, and moves people from soul to spirit, from focusing on circumstances to focusing on God.
- ✓ Strives to unify people and atmospheres with God and with one another, and brings messages of hope, encouragement, and joy.
- ✓ Demonstrates feet shod with the preparation of the gospel of peace and the good news of the gospel.
- ✓ Touches individuals, families, communities, and nations with an anointing that brings life changes.
- ✓ Pioneers and governs evangelistic works for God's glory.

# PASTORAL OFFICE

Let me begin by sharing some statistics regarding a traditional church pastor – not a pastoral office – but a traditional church pastor. These statistics will reveal the needful importance of SHIFTING from a pastoral paradigm to a fivefold ministry paradigm. Prayerfully after reading the statistics, those partake of this manual will have a new honor and respect for traditional pastors; also as they SHIFT into fivefold ministry, they will not want or bestow this paradigm upon those in the office of a pastor.

*Newly Revised Statistics Copyright 2018 - Statistics provided by The Fuller Institute, George Barna, Lifeway, Schaeffer Institute of Leadership Development, and Pastoral Care Inc.*

72% of the pastors report working between 55 to 75 hours per week.

84% of pastors feel they are on call 24/7.

80% believe pastoral ministry has negatively affected their families. Many pastor's children do not attend church now because of what the church has done to their parents.

65% of pastors feel their family lives in a "glass house" and fear they are not good enough to meet expectations.

23% of pastors report being distant to their family.

78% of pastors report having their vacation and personal time interrupted with ministry duties or expectations.

65% of pastors feel they have not taken enough vacation time with their family over the last 5 years.

28% of pastors report having feelings of guilt for taking personal time off and not telling the church.

35% of pastors report the demands of the church denies them from spending time with their family.

24% of pastor's families resent the church and its effect on their family.

22% of pastor's spouses reports the ministry places undue expectations on their family.

66% of church members expect a minister and family to live at a higher moral standard than themselves.

Moral values of a Christian is no different than those who consider themselves as non-Christians.

The average American will tell 23 lies a day.

53% of pastors report that the seminary did not prepare them for the ministry.

90% of pastors report the ministry was completely different than what they thought it would be like before they entered the ministry.

45% of pastors spend 10-15 hours a week on sermon preparation.

85% of pastors report the use of the internet and other resources have improved their study time compared to when they first started their ministry.

50% of pastors state they spend 1 hour in prayer each day.

95% of pastors report not praying daily or regularly with their spouse.

57% of pastors believe they do not receive a livable wage.

57% of pastors being unable to pay their bills.

53% of pastors are concerned about their future family financial security.

75% of pastors report significant stress-related crisis at least once in their ministry.

80% of pastors and 84% of their spouses have felt unqualified and discouraged in the role of pastors at least one or more times in their ministry.

52% of pastors feel overworked and cannot meet their church's unrealistic expectations.

54% of pastors find the role of a pastor overwhelming.

40% report serious conflict with a parishioner at least once in the last year.

80% of pastors expect conflict within their church.

75% of pastors report spending 4-5 hours a week in needless meetings.

35% of pastors battle depression or fear of inadequacy.

26% of pastors report being over fatigued.

28% of pastors report they are spiritually undernourished.

Over 50% of pastors state the biggest challenge is to recruit volunteers and encourage their members to change (living closer to God's Word).

70% of pastors report they have a lower self-image now than when they first started.

70% of pastors do not have someone they consider to be a close friend.

27% of pastors report not having anyone to turn to for help in a crisis situation.

81% of pastors have been tempted to have inappropriate sexual thoughts or behavior with someone in the church but have resisted.

17% of pastors report inappropriately texting with a church member at some time in their ministry.

34% of pastors wrestle with the temptation of pornography or visits pornographic sites.

57% of pastors feel fulfilled but yet discouraged, stressed, and fatigued.

84% of pastors desire to have close fellowship with someone they can trust and confide with.

Over 50% of pastors are unhealthy, overweight, and do not exercise.

The profession of "Pastor" is near the bottom of a survey of the most-respected professions, just above "car salesman." Many denominations are reporting an "Empty Pulpit Crisis." They do not have a shortage of ministers but have a shortage of ministers desiring to fill the role of a pastor.

71% of churches have no plan for a pastor to receive a periodic sabbatical.

66% of churches have no lay counseling support.

30% of churches have no documentation clearly outlining what the church expects of their pastor.

1 out of every 10 pastors will actually retire as a pastor.

**MY GOD! DELIVER AND SHIFT US AS A BODY OF CHRIST RIGHT NOW!**

One of the challenges we have in this day and age is that in an effort for apostles or vision leaders to avoid getting "stuck" in pastoral roles when leading a ministry that has Sunday services and typical church programs and structures, the minister who holds the office of a pastor is put in this position. Because there is little to no conscious governing of true fivefold culture, the ministry operates more in a pastoral paradigm and structure where the fivefold only manifests in measure. There may be free praise and worship is flowing which helps cultivate strong glory, gifts of the spirit may be in operation during these services, some members are established in their gifted fivefold offices, some trainings and teachings in fivefold ministry occur through workshops and conferences through the year, demons are cast out of people but principalities, territorial spirits, powers, and high places are not challenged within the region, so they still own the people, land, and territory. Many of the people are not empowered in their destiny and calling, still sit on the bench and watch a select few be used of the Lord, are encouraged by what is occurring in the ministry but are not fully discipled, built up, trained, and released in their destiny and calling. The pastor is often still overwhelmed in their shepherding duties as generally the only time the other offices assist with the sheep is when they are giving a prophetic word, praying during services, teaching or training, and initially assisting with drawing souls to salvation.

There is usually minimal teamwork in the area of governing the vision and shepherding as it is assumed this is role of the pastor. There is minimal ministry being done outside of the four walls of the church, so revival reformation is lacking as the sheep are encouraged to go outside the walks like they are in a pastoral paradigm, but are not sufficiently equipped in their destiny and calling to launch businesses, organizations, infiltrate systems. When the fivefold offices do go outside the four walls it is to minister to other ministries, not to impact their communities, regions, spheres, world and demonic systems. Many fivefold officers in this type of setting operate within the confines of the church and now on facebook, but have minimal impact or focus to transform their own region. This reinstitutes a pastoral paradigm in the guise of fivefold ministry. It also boxes the pastoral office into a religious and traditional role and lifestyle that is not the true fivefold mandate of their office. Speaking healing and a divine SHIFT into their true calling to those in the pastoral office right now in Jesus name. SHIFT!

Because of what I stated above, the stigma around falling pastors, and the increased new age attacks against the constitution of the church, many with the office of a pastor dread being identified. They are like "I just came out of traditional church mindsets and positions, now you want to stick me back there." If they have any wells or leadings in the other giftings and offices, then they strive to be identified in those areas, rather than being positioned in their pastoral office. It is essential that if we are going to restore true fivefold ministry, we make sure we are properly positioning and doing right by our pastoral officers.

<u>Pastor</u> in the Strong's Concordance means:
1. A shepherd
2. A herdsman
3. In the parable, he to whose care and control others have committed themselves, and whose precepts they follow
4. Of the overseers of the Christian assemblies
5. The task of the Near Eastern shepherd were; to watch for enemies trying to attack the sheep- to defend the sheep from attackers- to heal the wounded and sick sheep- to find and save lost or trapped sheep- to love them, sharing their lives and so earning their trust

<u>Shepherd</u> in dictionary.com:
1. A person who herds, tends, and guards sheep
2. A person who protects, guides, or watches over a person or group of people

A pastor is one who shepherds, oversees, cares for, and seeks to protect those who they minister too. The focus of their office is to provide guidance and wise direction that will aid the people in following the Lord. They display what to do and what not to do through their message, lifestyles while advising the people in making godly decisions and living godly lives.

Pastors may be responsible for preaching the regular ministry services, leading or supporting department heads within different programs of the ministry, overseeing or leading home or community groups, assisting in duties related to weddings, funerals, visitations, prayer, emergency and brief counseling, and other ministerial capacities. I will say that all who operate in the office of a pastor do not have the professional education to effectively counsel in-depth cases. Also, a pastor's role is not to be conducting long term counseling with members. At no time is an Army, Marine, Air Force officer sitting in a platoon, barracks, office, etc., continuously counseling someone they oversee. If that person is found to need such services, they are sent to the proper parties, and can even be placed on leave so they can receive the sufficient help and attention they need. I think this is where we tend to overwhelm the pastoral office. We expect them to deal with every problem, even those who require a processing to wholeness. As we love the analogy of the shepherd that leaves the flock to go get the one lost sheep, but the truth is if that shepherd d to keep going after that sheep, he is putting the rest of his flock in danger because his assignment is to the entire flock.

A pastor is to govern in his position and even to delegate with wisdom. He or she should be able and available to steward his duties properly. These cases should be sent to a professionally educated Christian counselor that has been identified with the ministry or referred to a counselor within the community. Members who require continuous attention and processing should be released to the proper mentors and counselors who have the time to effectively journey with them to wholeness. A pastor does not have the time for this, nor is this their calling. This is the reason traditional pastors are burned out; they are taking on duties that should be delegated out to the team mandate of fivefold ministry.

The pastoral's office legislates through the watchman, protection, covering, and empowerment authorities of God. Pastoral officers contend against sins and transgressions of the people, land, and region. They aim to protect people from the deceptions and demonic operations that would intend to harm their lives and draw them away from Christ. They minister messages and engage in operations that break people free from principalities, powers, spiritual wickedness that keep people bound personally, generationally, and regionally. They assert authority through there watchman ad shepherding office over demonic forces that keep people, lands, and regions, imprisoned, cycling, and hindered in their ability to be fully discipled. Pastoral officers embody and exude the heart, compassion, and love of God, which serve as weapons for annihilating darkness. They are very people oriented, and there is a strong level of personal connection, and intimacy they desire to have with people and legislate through that gives them sovereign authority to proclaim into the lives of those they govern and produce transformation. They speak direct messages that provide leadership, guidance, direction, advice, and care that will not only bless the people but cause them to follow after what God is speaking through them.

> *Acts 20:28-29 The Amplified Bible Take care and be on guard for yourselves and for the whole flock over which the Holy Spirit has appointed you as overseers, to shepherd (tend, feed, guide) the church of God which He bought with His own blood. I know that after I am gone, [false teachers like] ferocious wolves will come in among you, not sparing the flock;*
>
> *Isaiah 40:11 The Amplified Bible He will protect His flock like a shepherd, He will gather the lambs in His arm, He will carry them in His bosom; He will gently and carefully lead those nursing their young.*

Their messages nurture and cultivate the people they shepherd. The shepherding grace is embedded within their identity, character, nature, and purpose of their ministry. They may use dramatizations, props, and storylines to bring the fullness of their message across and provide the people with a visual display of God's word and will for them.

> *Ezekiel 34:11-16 The Amplified Bible For thus says the Lord God, "Behold, I Myself will search for My flock and seek them out. As a shepherd cares for his sheep on the day that he is among his scattered flock, so I will care for My sheep; and I will rescue them from all the places to which they were scattered on a cloudy and gloomy day. I will bring them out from the nations and gather them from the countries and bring them to their own land; and I will feed them on the mountains of Israel, by the streams, and in all the inhabited places of the land. I will feed them in a good pasture, and their grazing ground will be on the mountain heights of Israel. There they will lie down on good grazing ground and feed in rich pasture on the mountains of Israel. I will feed My flock and I will let them lie down [to rest]," says the Lord God. "I will seek the lost, bring back the scattered, bandage the crippled, and strengthen the weak and the sick; but I will destroy the fat and the strong [who have become hard-hearted and perverse]. I will feed them with judgment and punishment.*
>
> *Luke 15:3-7 The Amplified Bible So He told them this parable: "What man among you, if he has a hundred sheep and loses one of them, does not leave the ninety-nine in the wilderness and go after the one which is lost, [searching] until he finds it? And when he has found it, he lays it on his shoulders, rejoicing. And when he gets home, he calls together his friends and his neighbors, saying to them, 'Rejoice with me, because I have found my lost sheep!' I tell you, in the same way there will be more*

*joy in heaven over one sinner who repents than over ninety-nine righteous people who have no need of repentance.*

Pastors seek and search after the people, such that they can impact the wounded, strengthen the weak, and release a message to the lost. Just like Jesus, each sheep (person) is important to them, and they feel the urgency to make them a priority.

***Psalms 78:70-72 The Amplified Bible** He also chose David His servant And took him from the sheepfolds; From tending the ewes with nursing young He brought him To shepherd Jacob His people, And Israel His inheritance. So David shepherded them according to the integrity of his heart; And guided them with his skillful hands.*

***Jeremiah 3:15 The Amplified Bible** "Then [in the final time] I will give you [spiritual] shepherds after My own heart, who will feed you with knowledge and [true] understanding.*

Pastors have the heart, integrity, and ardor of God to feed and pour into the people. They are skilled specifically to provide spiritual guidance, knowledge, and understanding in the ways of God.

***Psalms 23:1-6 The Amplified Bible***

*The Lord is my Shepherd [to feed, to guide and to shield me]* **Pastors minister nourishment, guidance, and protection** *I shall not want.*

*He lets me lie down in green pastures; He leads me beside the still and quiet waters.* **Pastors minister safety and rest in God, peace, and tranquility.**

*He refreshes and restores my soul (life); He leads me in the paths of righteousness for His name's sake.* **Pastors minister life refreshing and restoration to the souls of people. Their ministry leads to paths of righteousness and godliness.**

*Even though I walk through the [sunless] valley of the shadow of death, I fear no evil, for You are with me; Your rod [to protect] and Your staff [to guide], they comfort and console me.* **Pastors minister encouragement and empowerment to prevail through all seasons of life. They provide comfort, love, and consolation.**

*You prepare a table before me in the presence of my enemies. You have anointed and refreshed my head with oil; My cup overflows. Surely goodness and mercy and unfailing love shall follow me all the days of my life, And I shall dwell forever [throughout all my days] in the house and in the presence of the Lord.* **Pastors release fresh anointing that brings overflowing replenishment. They seek to keep the people established in God's truth, attributes, and blessings that follow with having a relationship with Jesus Christ.**

## *Pastoral Officer Qualities*

- ✓ Reveal the mysteries of God's word and kingdom.
- ✓ Feed the sheep of God.
- ✓ Provides biblical principles to build faith and maturity.
- ✓ Provides a specific message that feeds the soul and spirit of the people and imparts revelation of who Christ is to us and our reasoning for being saved.
- ✓ Yields a biblical impartation.
- ✓ Has a heart of compassion; seeks to cover, protect, and guard the people.
- ✓ Provides some facet of covering for the people who are receiving from it.
- ✓ Seeks to lead, set the example, and minister messages of care and concern for the people.

## **TEACHERS OFFICE**

*Teach* in Dictionary.com means, "*To impart knowledge of or skill in; give instruction in.*"

The *Ephesians 4* mandate is to:

- ❖ Equip the saints
- ❖ Build up the body of Christ in unity and knowledge
- ❖ Bring maturity and the fullness of Christ such that God's children are no longer subject to deception by crafty demonic schemes

When a teacher officiates, they are equipping and building the people, ministry, community, and region, in the instruction, knowledge, intellect, wisdom, revelations, TRUTH, and mysteries of God. TEACHERS ARE TRUTH BEARERS. They do not teach their opinions, but God's facts ad analysis. They impart knowledge and skills to encourage, empower, and direct their audience or sphere in living a Christ-like life. They legislate authority by overseeing the educational and training capacities of ministries, businesses, and organizations, including writing and developing curriculum and performing teaching and training duties.

> ***Titus 2:7-8 New Living Bible*** *And you yourself must be an example to them by doing good works of every kind. Let everything you do reflect the integrity and seriousness of your teaching. Teach the truth so that your teaching can't be criticized. Then those who oppose us will be ashamed and have nothing bad to say about us.*

To be effective, the teacher must apply the instruction to their own lives and be an example of the truth. As they emulate the truth, their teaching cannot be criticized. Impartation occurs because they sow the revelation they carry into others. This is why it is important for them to reflect and live by what they minister and govern within their office, so their instructional impartation will be pure, evident, and unable to be opposed. Their ministry is revelatory and contains great clarity so that those who receive can easily learn and be enlightened.

> ***1Timothy 4:11 New Living Bible*** *Teach these things and insist that everyone learn them.*

<u>Teach in the Strong's Concordance means:</u>
1. To hold discourse with others in order to instruct them, deliver didactic discourses
2. Instill doctrine into one
3. The thing taught or enjoined
4. To explain or expound a thing
5. To teach one something

The teacher SHIFT and govern through their godly communication and dialogue. They instill godly doctrine, enjoining the message of God, and expound on the ideologies of God, thus convicting and transforming the hearts and minds of the people. They are assertive, firm, and commanding as they require an aligning with the instruction God is relaying.

> ***Psalm 32:8 The Amplified Bible*** *I will instruct you and teach you in the way you should go; I will counsel you [who are willing to learn] with My eye upon you.*

> ***Exodus 18:20 The Amplified Bible*** *You shall teach them the decrees and laws. You shall show them the way they are to live and the work they are to do.*

> ***1Thessalonians 4:1-2 The Amplified Bible*** *Finally, believers, we ask and admonish you in the Lord Jesus, that you follow the instruction that you received from us about how you ought to walk and please God (just as you are actually doing) and that you excel even more and more [pursuing a life of purpose and living in a way that expresses gratitude to God for your salvation]. For you know what commandments and precepts we gave you by the authority of the Lord Jesus.*

Their instruction gives direction and shows the people the way they should go to follow Jesus and live in a manner that is pleasing to Him. Their teaching brings encouragement and empowerment to help people progress on their course with God. They provide life lessons that people can connect with and receive a personal, relatable message. When they teach, they inspire, ignite, and stir the minds of the people to come up higher in the knowledge and revelation of Christ. They are skilled in stripping false mindsets, breaking down religious, deceptive, bewitched and bondage mind frames, and reforming minds in the true doctrine and ways of God. Teachers are scholars of the word and know how to utilize the scripture to change and restore minds. Teachers are really paradigm creators, and God can have them studying and teaching on a specific topic for months or years to break people and regions open to receive the true kingdom mind, will, and truth of God. They are a much needed part of the body of Christ as there are some spirits, ways of thinking and behaving that people, culture and ethnic groups, regions, communities, and generations that cannot be cast out by deliverance and prayer alone. They must be taught out and reformed in the knowledge, revelation, and character of Christ. They are activators who ignite, trigger, and mobilize the people in the direction of God.

Those in the office of a teacher contend against demonic powers and vain imaginations that attempt to exalt themselves against the knowledge and kingdom of God. They correct, rebuke, convict, and expose ungodly truths, error, mixture, flightiness, falsehoods, counterfeits, haughty, and foolish wisdom. Their main purpose is to keep people from being destroyed through faulty, prideful and wicked doctrines and imaginations.

> ***1Corinthians 1:27*** *But God hath chosen the foolish things of the world to confound the wise; and God hath chosen the weak things of the world to confound the things which are mighty.*

> *Proverbs 16:18* *Pride goeth before destruction, and an haughty spirit before a fall.*
>
> *2Corinthians 10:4-5* *(For the weapons of our warfare are not carnal, but mighty through God to the pulling down of strong holds;) Casting down imaginations, and every high thing that exalteth itself against the knowledge of God, and bringing into captivity every thought to the obedience of Christ; And having in a readiness to revenge all disobedience, when your obedience is fulfilled.*
>
> *Romans 8:37-39* *Nay, in all these things we are more than conquerors through him that loved us. For I am persuaded, that neither death, nor life, nor angels, nor principalities, nor powers, nor things present, nor things to come, Nor height, nor depth, nor any other creature, shall be able to separate us from the love of God, which is in Christ Jesus our Lord.*

Powers are high ranking supernatural demons or demonic influences that cause evil and sin in the world. Powers are those who operate in positions of influence much like teachers to control, possess, confuse, sway, and transform the minds, beliefs, and standards of people. Powers seek to implement alternative doctrines that are self-focused, people focused, or demonic focused. There mandate is idolatry – exchanging the worship of the creature for creation.

> *Romans 1:22-26* *Professing themselves to be wise, they became fools, And changed the glory of the uncorruptible God into an image made like to corruptible man, and to birds, and fourfooted beasts, and creeping things. Wherefore God also gave them up to uncleanness through the lusts of their own hearts, to dishonour their own bodies between themselves: Who changed the truth of God into a lie, and worshipped and served the creature more than the Creator, who is blessed for ever. Amen. For this cause God gave them up unto vile affections: for even their women did change the natural use into that which is against nature:*

Powers engage in this demonic authority through the legislation of demonic teachings, misguided inferences, opinions, explorations, impressions, and considerations, culture trends, enactment demonic policies and laws that appear to be good and what is best for people, lands, or regions, yet separate and sway them from the will, plans, purposes, and standards of God. Teaching officers cast these powers down. Teaching officers contend against powers in warfare, intercession, instruction, proclamation, scribing curriculum while sounding the alarm in communities and systems, and educating the people in the truths and ways of God.

Like Jesus, who often taught rather than preached and was known as a teacher, heavenly signs and wonders should follow teaching officers. Those in the teaching office can be the most boring teacher, yet manifest signs. Paul had an experience where someone fell asleep due to his boring teaching, but because he governed his office, he raised him back to life.

> *Acts 20:9-12* *And there sat in a window a certain young man named Eutychus, being fallen into a deep sleep: and as Paul was long preaching, he sunk down with sleep, and fell down from the third loft, and was taken up dead. And Paul went down, and fell on him, and embracing him said, Trouble not yourselves; for his life is in him. When he therefore was come up again, and had broken bread, and eaten, and talked a long while, even till break of day, so he departed. And they brought the young man alive, and were not a little comforted.*

Teaching officers are not bound to the four walls of the church. They can teach anywhere God leads them. They teach in personal conversation and to large groups. Their nature is to instruct and turn hearts to God their father. Jesus taught everywhere the instruction of God was needed. Even his prayers, deliverances, and healings, was accompanied instruction where others could learn and be like him, as Jesus made sure the kingdom manifested as he commanded the kingdom of heaven to come forth – SHIFT forth – through his very life, actions, and teaching.

> *Matthew 4:23* *Jesus was going throughout all Galilee, teaching in their synagogues and proclaiming the gospel of the kingdom, and healing every kind of disease and every kind of sickness among the people.*

> *Matthew 7:28-29* *And it came to pass, when Jesus had ended these sayings, the people were astonished at his doctrine: For he taught them as one having authority, and not as the scribes.*

> *Mark 4:2* *And He was teaching them many things in parables, and was saying to them in His teaching,*

> *Mark 6:34* *When Jesus went ashore, He saw a large crowd, and He felt compassion for them because they were like sheep without a shepherd; and He began to teach them many things.*

*Luke 4:15 And He began teaching in their synagogues and was praised by all.*

*Luke 5:3 And He got into one of the boats, which was Simon's, and asked him to put out a little way from the land. And He sat down and began teaching the people from the boat.*

*John 3:2 This man came to Jesus by night and said to Him, "Rabbi, we know that You have come from God as a teacher; for no one can do these signs that You do unless God is with him."*

*John 7:14 But when it was now the midst of the feast Jesus went up into the temple, and began to teach.*

*John 8:2 Early in the morning He came again into the temple, and all the people were coming to Him; and He sat down and began to teach them.*

*2John 1:9 Anyone who goes too far and does not abide in the teaching of Christ, does not have God; the one who abides in the teaching, he has both the Father and the Son.*

## *Homework Explorations:*

1. Share in detail what you learned about each fivefold operation.
2. Share with fivefold operation you believe you operate in and why?
3. Journal your thoughts about the pastoral statistics.
4. Write a letter of gratitude to pastors. Post it on your facebook page.
5. Journal regarding two people you know operate in two of these offices and what you learned about their office.
6. What reasons are these offices important to the body of Christ? To the world?
7. As you consider your current ministry, how can you all improve in operating in these fivefold offices?
8. Journal how you would explain the fivefold offices to someone who felt they were not for today.
9. Journal how you would explain the fivefold offices to an unbeliever.
10. Spend time in prayer thanking God for the fivefold gifts he left in the earth. Journal your experience.

# FIVEFOLD SPIRITUAL GIFTS

- ✓ The Holy Spirit distributes different spiritual gifts to the believer.
- ✓ We can ask the Holy Spirit to give us these gifts, and he can teach us how to operate in them.
- ✓ As we grow in these gifts, we can become skilled in using them.
- ✓ We are also born with distinct gifts and talents that empower our destiny and calling. These gifts help us to identify how the anointing operates in our lives, what anointing wells our callings flow through, what our metron is, and who our remnant is.

> *Romans 12:6-8 Having then gifts differing according to the grace that is given to us, whether prophecy, let us prophesy according to the proportion of faith; Or ministry, let us wait on our ministering: or he that teacheth, on teaching; Or he that exhorteth, on exhortation: he that giveth, let him do it with simplicity; he that ruleth, with diligence; he that sheweth mercy, with cheerfulness.*

> *1Corinthians 12: 8-10 Now there are diversities of gifts, but the same Spirit. And there are differences of administrations, but the same Lord. And there are diversities of operations, but it is the same God which worketh all in all. But the manifestation of the Spirit is given to every man to profit withal. For to one is given by the Spirit the word of wisdom; to another the word of knowledge by the same Spirit; For to one is given by the Spirit the word of wisdom; to another the word of knowledge by the same Spirit; To another faith by the same Spirit; to another the gifts of healing by the same Spirit; To another the working of miracles; to another prophecy; to another discerning of spirits; to another divers kinds of tongues; to another the interpretation of tongues:*

---

*These gifts help us to identify how the anointing operates in our lives, what anointing wells our callings flow through, what our metron is, and who our remnant is.*

---

> *1Corinthians 12:28-31 And God hath set some in the church, first apostles, secondarily prophets, thirdly teachers, after that miracles, then gifts of healings, helps, governments, diversities of tongues. Are all apostles? are all prophets? are all teachers? are all workers of miracles? Have all the gifts of healing? do all speak with tongues? do all interpret?*

*But covet earnestly the best gifts: and yet shew I unto you a more excellent way.*

**Diversities of Gifts** *entail the different gifts of the Holy Spirit.*

**Differences of Administrations** *are the distinct authorities and governmental execution of the gifts. We each have a different measure of authority in how a gift will consistently or tangibly manifests.*

**Diversities of operations** *are distinct ways to which the gifts work through our God identity. Because of the unique images of God we possess, we each will have unique ways of manifesting the gifts of the Holy Spirit*

Gifts of the Holy Spirit are as followed:

- *Word of Wisdom* - God's supernatural perspective on how to achieve His will and purpose. God's knowledge rightly applied to specific situations.
- *Word of Knowledge* - "Facts" given by God that are unknowable without spiritual revelation.
- *The Gift of Faith* - The supernatural ability to believe God without doubt. Essential to the Gift of Healing and Miracles.
- *The Gifts of Healing* - Supernatural healing through special anointing wells of the Holy Spirit. Healings can manifest through teaching, preaching, prophecy, word of knowledge, laying on of hands, deliverance, soul, heart, mind, and identity healing, emotional healing, and counseling.
- *The Working of Miracles* - A supernatural display of power, signs, and wonders that goes beyond the natural to counteract earthly and evil forces.
- *Discerning of Spirits* - Spiritual insight into differences between the Holy Spirit, the spirit of man, and evil spirits at work in the earth; it is not the discerning of character faults or flaws. This revelation manifests through the spiritual senses and/or one's knower. It is the ability to judge, explore, know, consider, and reveal truth through the spirit of God. It is not from the natural realm or emotions as that is more superstition or intuition than godly discernment
- *The Gift of Prophecy* - The forth-telling of God's utterance. It is not of the intellect but of the Spirit. It is divinely inspired and anointed words spoken, song, or worked by a believer.
- *Divers Kinds of Tongues* - This is not to be confused with the use of tongues in private prayer or worship. This refers to the ministry of

tongues to others. An utterance from a believer to another in a language unknown to the speaker. *(Isaiah 28:11; Mark 16:17; Acts 2:4; 10:44-48; 19:1-7; 1Corinthians 12:10; 13:1-3; 14:2, 4-22, 26-31; 28:31)*
- ➤ *Interpretation of Tongues* - Supernatural power to reveal the meaning of tongues. Not a translation, but an interpretation. Tongues and Interpretation working together can be the equivalent of prophecy.

## *Homework Exploration*
1. What fivefold ministry gifts do you already possess?
2. How does these gifts manifest through your destiny and calling
3. What gifts would you like to cultivate with the Holy Spirit? What reasons do you desire these gifts?
4. Consider two people you walk in ministry with. What gifts do they possess and how do they compare to the flow of your gifts?
5. What are the benefits of these spiritual gifts consistently flowing in a ministry?
6. Spend time googling and studying more in-depth on each gift. Journal a few scriptures also reference and other revelation you learned about them.
7. Spend time seeking the Holy Spirit for more of his presence and operation of the spiritual gifts. Journal your experiences.

# SHIFTING FROM GIFTS TO CALLING

The most essential SHIFT anyone coming into fivefold ministry will have to take is SHIFTING from gifting to calling.

- Many people in the world attend schools, colleges, work jobs, engage in social service acts, and participate in activities, because of what they do well.
- Many people within a traditional church setting are positioned within the ministry because of what they do well.
- Many are not brought up to think about destiny and often stumble into it by happenstance or engaging in what they do well.

Gifts are great and necessary. But a person can engage in their gifts but never operate in their calling. We often see this with Hollywood stars and famous athletes. They appear to love what they do, and make lots of money, but are discontent and lack fulfillment because their life is void of true purpose.

Many who manage to come into their calling without a relationship with God experience void or they end up offering their lives up to the god of the world or a demonic God. There are even those within the body of Christ who serve God, experience minimal fulfillment because they do not know their true calling and how God's identity is to be released in the earth through them. It is important that we not only do something well, but also live a life of purpose. Purpose reveals our calling. Our calling is revealed through our God identity, which entails our unique blueprint for the reason we were born into the world.

Dictionary.com defines "*Identity*" as:
1. the state or fact of remaining the same one or ones, as under varying aspects or conditions
2. the condition of being oneself or itself, and not another
3. condition or character as to who a person or what a thing is
4. the state or fact of being the same one as described
5. the sense of self, providing sameness and continuity in personality over time
6. exact likeness in nature or qualities: an identity of interests
7. an instance or point of sameness or likeness

**Basically, our identity defines:**

- Who we are

- Who we are not
- Who we belong to
- What we are a part of
- What our character and nature is
- What our belief systems are
- Who we were born to be

**When God created us:**
- He first made us in His likeness and resemblance
- Releases a blessing over His creation
- Prophesied into what He made

> *Genesis 1:26-28 And God said, Let us make man in our image, after our likeness: and let them have dominion over the fish of the sea, and over the fowl of the air, and over the cattle, and over all the earth, and over every creeping thing that creepeth upon the earth. So God created man in his own image, in the image of God created he him; male and female created he them. And God blessed them, and God said unto them, Be fruitful, and multiply, and replenish the earth, and subdue it: and have dominion over the fish of the sea, and over the fowl of the air, and over every living thing that moveth upon the earth.*

Our calling resides in how God uniquely designed us to impact the earth as we live in dominion through the authority he has given us in the earth. It is difficult to know our true calling and live fulfilled in life apart from God. This is because we are created in his image. We need his leading and relationship with him to get to know what part of himself he has put in us, and how we are to SHIFT the world with it.

---

*It is difficult to know our true calling and live fulfilled in life apart from God.*

---

*Ephesians 4:12* tells us that fivefold ministry is for the perfecting and full equipping of the saints, to work towards the building up of the body of Christ. When building is occurring or even when a building is being built, it is for specific purpose. Building occurs and buildings are built for destiny. The architect designs it to do just what it needs to do and it is built for that purpose. The only way to perfect and fully equip the saints toward building the body is for them to know their calling. This will perfect them in the identity and destiny the Lord has ordained for their lives. There is, therefore, no way to effectively walk in true fivefold ministry without developing, training, equipping, and releasing people in their destiny and calling; as you will not just be serving God, but living and learning a life of purpose in him.

> *John 15:16 You did not choose me, but I chose you and appointed you so that you might go and bear fruit – fruit that will last – and so that whatever you ask in my name the Father will give you.*

**When we and others acknowledge our calling, an unveiling and unmasking of what was already identified, imparted, blessed, and prophesied begin to manifest.**

- *God revealed Joseph's calling to him in a dream -* **Genesis 37**
- *God revealed Sampson's calling to his mother before his birth –* **Judges 13:5**
- *God revealed Jeremiah's calling to him -* **Jeremiah 1:5**
- *David declared and sang the fear and wonder of his calling to God* **Psalms 139:13-16**
- *Isaiah spoke God's words over himself regarding his own calling -* **Isaiah 49:1-3**
- *As prophesied regarding John the Baptist's calling -* **Luke 1:15**
- *As prophesied regarding Jesus' calling -* **Isaiah 9:6**
- *Jesus made Peter agree three times to walk in his destiny –* **John 21:17**
- *Paul's true calling unveiled on the road to Demarcus even though he already thought he was doing destiny* **Acts 9:3-9**

*Let's explore Jesus SHIFTING the disciples from giftings to callings.*

> *Matthew 4:18-20 And Jesus, walking by the sea of Galilee, saw two brethren, Simon called Peter, and Andrew his brother, casting a net into the sea: for they were fishers. And he saith unto them, Follow me, and I will make you fishers of men. And they straightway left their nets, and followed him.*

The first SHIFT the disciples took was to lay down their nets – what they did well, what they knew well, what they thought was their destiny and calling – and followed Jesus. They also SHIFTED to allowing Jesus to define their purpose. Jesus told them what they would do in life. Not their momma, daddy, teacher, pastor, leader, society. JESUS DEFINED THEIR CALLING! You have to make this SHIFT too if you are going to know true purpose. SHIFT!

As Jesus SHIFTED the disciples, their focus became not just about making money, or themselves, but their focus became people focused and God focused, and how they could transform lives for God's glory. You will also have to SHIFT in your scope regarding your life where it is not about you but about others and the God in you, as this is true purpose. SHIFT!

The disciples SHIFTING with Jesus revealed that they had a desire to live for him, had a desire to learn and live in relationship with him, and had a desire to be leaders in his kingdom. You have to want what God has ordained for your life. You have to even want to lead and be an example of Jesus Christ; and regardless of your purpose, you have to want to be a minister of the gospel for Jesus. SHIFT!

The disciples walked daily with Jesus. Their calling SHIFTED into a lifestyle. They SHIFTED into covenant relationship with one another and with Jesus. Jesus's very life and actions taught them character, ministry, steadfastness, fervency in preaching the gospel and how to go where the fish where. Jesus perfected and equipped them through teaching and hands on training. Jesus deprogrammed, reprogrammed and redefined the disciples, such that fishing was not just a gift, but a purposed way of life. You will also have to journey with Jesus and those he sends to perfect and equip you. You will have to be redefined in understanding purpose and living it as a way of life.

Here is a list of some teachings and equipping keys Jesus imparted into the disciples.

*From By Ron Sider – Adapted from an interview for Turning Toward Jesus video curriculum. Sider is a professor of theology from Philadelphia, Pa. (Website http://thirdway.com/love-jesus/key-teachings/)*

- The Christian life is marked by baptism (Matt. 3:13-17).adult baptism
- God is available to help us not give in to temptation (Matt. 4:1-11).
- Jesus asks us to repent—turn away from wrong, confess wrongdoing (Matt. 4:17).

- Jesus says, "Follow me" and you will help find other followers (Matt. 4:18-22).
- Jesus says, "Take up your cross and follow me" (Matt. 16:24-27).
- Repeatedly Jesus notes, "The kingdom of heaven is at hand." Jesus seems to be telling us ways to experience heaven on earth now, and he also refers to a future realm where we will be in the presence of God and Jesus (Matt. 4:23; 13:18-52; 18:1-5).
- Jesus showed compassion for all and helped them: the poor, the despised, the outcasts, and wants us to do the same (Matt. 4:24-25;9:9-13).
- Jesus says he is like "new wineskins" or a completely new thing (Matt. 9:14-17).
- The many stories and healings of Jesus teach us, "Have faith; it is enough" (Matt. 9:18-31).
- Jesus emphasizes, "Be sincere, not a hypocrite" (Matt. 6:1-6).
- Jesus and God are one (Matt. 10:40; 16:13-20).
- Jesus warns, "Don't let family get in the way of following me" (Matt. 10:35-38; 12:46-50).
- Jesus has authority over the law and tradition (Matt. 12: 1-8; 15:1-9).
- Jesus fulfills Old Testament scriptures (Matt. 1:22-23; 17:9-13).
- Jesus preaches, "Love your enemies; do not hate, be reconciled" (Matt. 5:38-48; 5:21-24).
- Jesus reminds us, "You must become like a child to enter the kingdom" (Matt. 19:13-15).
- Jesus' disciples become a community of faith, which forms the beginnings of the Christian church universal (Matt. 28:16-19).
- The events of Jesus' last week on earth are the culmination of his ministry and teachings, climaxing with his death on the cross. A man who has never sinned dies to save all the rest of us who have sinned (Matt. 21-27).
- Jesus says, "I am alive! Go and tell everyone else" (Matt. 28:7-10).
- He adds, "I will be with you forever" (Matt. 28:20b).

As Jesus taught and equipped them, he charged them to SHIFT into going into the cities and regions and operating in ministry. They could not be comfortable in just watching him minister, co-laboring with him as he ministered, or sitting around and doing nothing. Fivefold ministry has to be alive, active, and operating through you to produce your destiny and calling. SHIFT!

> *Matthew 10:6-7 These twelve Jesus sent forth, and commanded them, saying, Go not into the way of the Gentiles, and into any city of the*

> *Samaritans enter ye not: But go rather to the lost sheep of the house of Israel. And as ye go, preach, saying, The kingdom of heaven is at hand.*

As Jesus charged them, he did not send them forth in gifts and talents. He commissioned them and SHIFTED them forth as ministers - preachers of the gospel - and eventually as fivefold officers. The gifts were innate and a part of the calling upon their lives. Among the disciples stood apostles, prophets, evangelists, pastors, teachers. All carrying their unique mantle and authoritative ranking, and skilled in their perspective giftings, yet having one common goal - to preach the kingdom.

> *Matthew 28:17-19 Then the eleven disciples went away into Galilee, into a mountain where Jesus had appointed (commissioned) them. And when they saw him, they worshipped him: But some doubted. And Jesus came and spake unto them, saying, All power is given unto me in heaven and in earth. Go ye therefore, and teach all nations, baptizing them in the name of the Father, and of the Son, and of the Holy Ghost: Teaching them to observe all things whatsoever I have commanded you: and, lo, I am with you alway, even unto the end of the world. Amen.*

**You have always been who God created you to be, so it is okay to embrace your destiny and calling, and SHIFT into being perfected, equipped, and built up in it.**

> ➤When you reject your identity and calling, you reject God in you, curse your inherited blessing, and alter or stunt the promises and prophecies that was spoken into your life before birth.
> ➤When you accept your identity and calling, you embrace God's image in you, reap your inherited blessings, and you are able to live and experience the promises and prophecies that was spoken into you before birth.

As you embrace, align, and are built inside your purpose, a continual unveiling of your calling unfolds as you journey with God in a destiny lifestyle.

> *2Corinthians 3:16-18 Nevertheless when it shall turn to the Lord, the vail shall be taken away. Now the Lord is that Spirit: and where the Spirit of the Lord is, there is liberty. But we all, with open face beholding as in a glass the glory of the Lord, are changed into the same image from glory to glory, even as by the Spirit of the Lord.*

This unveiling derives through the specific standards that God requires you to live by as you journey in a destiny lifestyle in him. We all have general godly principles and sound doctrine we abide by as a body of believers, but beholding your specific standards will solidify you in tranquil peace about who God created and called you to be, and what he has purposed for your life. Standards are not just morals and values, as morals and values can be good, decent, and respectful, but lack Godly principles and standards.

- ✓ Standards are tailor made biblical principles that align with the word of God, while enabling you to hold fast the profession of your faith. Standards keep you from transgressing against the character, nature, virtue, maturity, discipline, faith, steadfastness, and governmental authority God is requiring your life.
- ✓ Standards provide you with the stamina and fortification to successfully carry the mantle, giftings, calling, and kingdom office of God. Though some characteristics are similar, some authorities, abilities, capabilities, and mandates are very different and therefore, require particular standards to fulfill its purpose.
- ✓ These intricate standards enable you to strategically be the unique blueprint God has designed you to be even though others may share the same gifts, callings, positions, offices, spheres as you do.
- ✓ You must know and respect your standards so you can maintain the purity, power, rulership, and identification needed to produce what God is mandating.
- ✓ The standards God require of you may be different than what God is requiring of someone else. You may think God's standards for someone else are more lenient or strict compared to yours. God knows your value, worth, tendencies, propensities, capacities, abilities. He will set standards to keep you safe and flourishing in your personal identity and God given blueprint.

Seek God for your specific standards and embrace them as a lifestyle. They will sustain you as you journey from level to level and glory to glory, in a destiny lifestyle with God. SHIFT!

### *Homework Explorations:*
1. Journal your thoughts regarding this chapter.
2. What are the differences between operating in gifts versus calling?
3. Journal on the gifts you possess.

4. Journal regarding what you believe your calling is? What has God said about what your calling is? How has others confirmed or resisted what God has said regarding your calling?
5. In what ways do you need to SHIFT from operating in giftings to calling?
6. Write a decree that entails your gifts, calling, and SHIFTING from gifts to calling.
7. What are the standards God is requiring of you, such that you sustain your journey in a successful destiny lifestyle with the Lord?

# MATURING INTO THE FIVEFOLD OFFICE

Most fivefold officers evolve into their seated calling. They may start their walk with God operating in their gifts as prophets, evangelists, pastors, etc., then as they accept their ministerial call and do the works, they begin to have hands on training with the Holy Spirit with being identified and SHIFTED into their seated office. Those Jesus commissioned as apostles where first disciples that journeyed with Jesus in learning various fivefold ministry works, then he SHIFTED them into the calling of seated fivefold officers when it was time.

> *Matthew 28:16-20* *Then the eleven disciples went away into Galilee, into a mountain where Jesus had appointed them. And when they saw him, they worshipped him: but some doubted. And Jesus came and spake unto them, saying, All power is given unto me in heaven and in earth. Go ye therefore, and teach all nations, baptizing them in the name of the Father, and of the Son, and of the Holy Ghost: Teaching them to observe all things whatsoever I have commanded you: and, lo, I am with you alway, even unto the end of the world. Amen.*

Most apostles go through a process of learning in the other fivefold offices and the operations of their gifts through those positions. They even walking in that office for a season before realizing and evolving into apostles. It is as if God teaches apostles the other seats first, so they can learn the identity, operations, training and equipping of those positions and what it takes to lead them since the apostle is the head of the fivefold ministry team.

Please understand and be okay that all teams have ahead - have a leader. For some reason, in the body of Christ, we hate to acknowledge this. Though we are all one body, though we are a team, someone has to lead the team to make sure it operates sufficiently. In fivefold ministry, the apostle is that person. If the apostle does not have the blueprint for the equipping of the team, purpose of the team, and the mandate that the team will release in the earth, then the team will not flourish. They will do some good works but not an apostolic work that really establishes the vision and kingdom of God in the earth.

Some people may start out in one office then as they grow, they SHIFT into another office. Many prophets experience this. Especially if they walk closely with apostles and endeavor in a lot of the inside workings that pertain to the office of an apostle. Silas in the Bible was a prophet who was appointed among the seventy sent forth in *Luke 10:1-2*.

> *After these things the Lord appointed other seventy also, and sent them two and two before his face into every city and place, whither he himself would come. Therefore said he unto them, The harvest truly is great, but the labourers are few: pray ye therefore the Lord of the harvest, that he would send forth labourers into his harvest.*

*Most fivefold officers evolve into their seated calling.*

- ✓ Silas was used as a fivefold ministry voice and emerged more of an apostle as he journeyed with Paul in ministry.

*Acts 15:22 Then pleased it the apostles and elders, with the whole church, to send chosen men of their own company to Antioch with Paul and Barnabas; namely, Judas surnamed Barsabas, and Silas, chief men among the brethren:*

*Acts 15:32 And Judas and Silas, being prophets also themselves, exhorted the brethren with many words, and confirmed them.*

*Acts 15:37-41 And Barnabas determined to take with them John, whose surname was Mark. But Paul thought not good to take him with them, who departed from them from Pamphylia, and went not with them to the work. And the contention was so sharp between them, that they departed asunder one from the other: and so Barnabas took Mark, and sailed unto Cyprus; And Paul chose Silas, and departed, being recommended by the brethren unto the grace of God. And he went through Syria and Cilicia, confirming the churches.*

Along with the Apostle Paul, Silas also journeyed and labored with Peter and Timothy who were also apostles. Silas is mention among Apostle Paul and Timothy in *1Thessalonians 1-2* in letter writings to the Thessalonian church. I encourage you to study his life as he is a great example of one maturing from on fivefold office to another (*Matthew 5:13-14, Acts 15-17 17, 2Corinthians 1:19, 1Peter 5:12*).

Sometimes a believer can have a well of another office but not necessarily govern in that office. Many evangelist have a prophetic well. This does not necessarily mean they govern in the office of a prophet. They may simply be a prophetic evangelist where God uses them prophetically to do the work of an evangelist. Many preachers or pastors have a prophetic or apostolic well but are not necessarily prophet and apostle officers. They have a strong gift and anointing that allows them to flow through that well to advance the kingdom of God. This is important to note because it occurs often, especially in this day and time where God has immeasurably poured out his spirit and the Holy Spirit is so tangible and assessable and where people are going after God with a vengeance (*Joel 2:28-32, Acts 2:17-18*).

In order to be viewed as operating in more than one office, you actually have to be able to GOVERN IN AUTHORITY in both areas. God has to literally give you an OFFICIATING SEAT in those offices. In this case, a leader would equip, train, and release you in both offices. An example of titles with both offices would be an apostolic prophet, a prophetic evangelist, a prophetic teacher, an apostolic pastor. You would eventually be given both office titles as you are ordained and released in those areas.

Maturity is very important in fivefold ministry. *Ephesians 4:13* lets us know that we must SHIFT into maturity as a person and as a minister. And we must be able to fully manifest the maturity of Christ in our daily walk with him.

> *Ephesians 4:13* Till we all come in the unity of the faith, and of the knowledge of the Son of God, unto a perfect man, unto the measure of the stature of the fulness of Christ:
>
> **The Amplified Bible** *[That it might develop] until we all attain oneness in the faith and in the comprehension of the [full and accurate] knowledge of the Son of God, that [we might arrive] at really mature manhood (the completeness of personality which is nothing less than the standard height of Christ's own perfection), the measure of the stature of the fullness of the Christ and the completeness found in Him.*

This means we must mature in:
- ✓ The application of labor and growth
- ✓ Mental and moral character
- ✓ Integrity and virtue
- ✓ Completeness in God as a person and as his child
- ✓ Whole in our mental, emotional, and physical state

- ✓ In our ability to produce, reproduce, and multiply what God has instilled in us and granted to our hands
- ✓ In our destiny and calling and ability to operate sufficiently and effectively
- ✓ Producing the kingdom of God in the earth
- ✓ Governing ourselves while representing a kingdom lifestyle
- ✓ Governing the ministry, offices, visions, and mandates granted to us

We have to want to be grown in Jesus and fully grown in what he has called us to do. With this understanding, we realize that we are constantly evolving. Even when we mature, we seek to mature again, such that we are always attaining the highest height Jesus is SHIFTING us to. When this is your posture, you will always grow with God. You will not build a high place and can SHIFT with him as he evolves you for his glory. This is important because you may think you have found your niche in destiny, in your vision, or even in your identity. God comes along and throws everything off by showing you where you may need to SHIFT, where there is more to a thing, where you need to expand, or where you need to mature or SHIFT in your character. Your posture has to be I LIVE IN THE SHIFT WITH GOD. I AM THE SHIFT OF GOD! That way, your comfortability is pleasing him, moving with him, and living in evolving destiny with him. I decree a SHIFT to this posture in you right now in Jesus name. SHIFT!

### *Homework Explorations:*
1. Journal in detail, your journey of maturity from an unbeliever to a believer and how the spiritual gifts and offices have manifested throughout your life.
2. Journal experiences where you needed to grow but was comfortable in your identity and lifestyle and was resistant to growing.
3. Journal experiences where God was SHIFTING you in ministry, but you were resistant to evolving with him.
4. Journal areas where you need to mature in your character and identity.
5. Journal areas where you need to mature in your ministry, destiny, and calling.
6. Journal in detail how God has used your gifts, talents, and the positions you have operated in to prepare you as a minister and/or fivefold office.

# LICENSING & ORDINATION

*Some of the revelation in this chapter is from Dr. Taquetta Baker's book, "The Apostolic Mantle."*

I chose to write on this topic because there is a lot of mixed emotions and messages regarding being licensed and ordained. Many have the mindset of "*I do not need a title.*" But truthfully you would not allow some to operate on you that did not have training, experience, and certified accreditation. Many use their title to control and abuse others, and there are some people who are validated by their title. Then there are the ones that are sinful and lack the character and nature of God until you want to strip them of their title. They have made it difficult for those of us who are humble and integral in wearing the label of the Lord.

We cannot allow personal insecurities and the challenge of being associated with those who misuse titles to shame or hinder us from wanting and pursing licensing and ordination and from setting up programs within our fivefold ministries to make sure people are licensed and ordained. If people who are truly submitted to God's will do not assert their right to be licensed and ordained, then how will the world know who the true Godly leaders are? We are trying to hide when we should be at the forefront of the body of Christ and kingdom boldly declaring with our lives, "This is what God's leader looks like." We have to stop allowing the discrepancies of some shame us into shining and boldly representing the very gospel we claim we love, serve, and live for.

As you grow in God, receiving licenses, ordinations, and certifications is a part of your reward. This is something God told me when I was being ordained. He said I was being rewarded and honored for my hard work and years of service, dedication, and maturity in him. He said he was proud of me, and it was a moment to be proud of myself. When we are in the worldly educational system or in our jobs, we obtain degrees, certificates, awards, certifications, and bonuses for our progress and success. This should be the same within the body of Christ, especially if we claim to be a fivefold ministry. A fivefold ministry is a training and equipping center. Some of these centers should be literal educational systems where people can obtain high school diplomas, professional degrees and certifications, and especially licenses and commissioning in their call and office. We should want to have an established accredited kingdom educational center where people are trained, equipped, honored, and sent forth in their call to preach the gospel of Jesus Christ. It is a religious false paradigm and mindset when we make people believe that they are sacrificing their lives and no blessing or honor comes with that - that it is our duty to serve God without recognition of our growth and success. But God's entire bible and even one of the main reasons he created us was so he could bless us. Jesus came so that we could be restored in the blessings of eternal life. We have to SHIFT from making this walk be all about dread and sacrifice and demonstrate the empowerment, grace, and productivity of the true kingdom of God.

> *Ephesians 4:11-13* states The Amplified Bible And His gifts were varied; He Himself appointed and gave men to us, some to be apostles (special messengers), some prophets (inspired preachers and expounders), some evangelists (preachers of the Gospel, traveling missionaries), some pastors (shepherds of His flock) and teachers. His intention was the perfecting and the full equipping of the saints (His consecrated people) that they should do the work of ministering toward building up Christ's body (the church). [That it might develop] until we all attain oneness in the faith and in the comprehension of the [full and accurate] knowledge of the Son of God, that [we might arrive] at really mature manhood (the completeness of personality which is nothing less than the standard height of Christ's own perfection), the measure of the stature of the fullness of the Christ and the completeness found in Him.

*Ordination helps establish and solidify the specific work, vision, and focus regarding the calling and mantle that is upon your life.*

Licensing proves you have been educated, trained, equipped, and given formal permission from a governmental or constituted authority to perform a work in a specific area. In the world, once you obtain a professional degree in a particular area, you have to take a test to acquire a license and then each year, you have to acquire a certain amount of educational credits to demonstrate that you are receiving continual education in your field of study. If you do not fulfill this requirement, you lose your license and right to legally work in your profession. I believe such a system should be established in fivefold ministries. Especially since *Ephesians 4:13* tells us that we should be perfected and equipped until we ALL attain oneness in the faith and can demonstrate full and accurate knowledge of the son of God. This scripture lets us know that we are continual learners of this great gospel. That there is an eternal evolving of learning Jesus Christ, how to walk with him in destiny, and how to journey in our call as his ministers.

When we considered being ordained as officers, we know that military officers in the world are given medallions, ribbons, and awards for their decorated services related to training, outstanding services, achievements, and heroisms. Many of their medallions can be pinned on their military uniform to demonstrate they are the military service they belong to, rank, outstanding services, and achievements. When they are dressed in their uniform and are displaying their medallions, they are given honor and respect everywhere they go for serving their country, for the great sacrifices they have made to fight for their country, and for the achievements they have accomplished. I believe in our effort to remain humbled, we have stripped the body of Christ from honoring and awarding one another for the sacrifices and achievements we make for the sake of the gospel. This needs to be restored as we aim to establish true fivefold ministries in the earth.

> *Matthew 10:1-8* *And when he had called unto him his twelve disciples, he gave them power against unclean spirits, to cast them out, and to heal all manner of sickness and all manner of disease. Now the names of the twelve apostles are these; The first, Simon, who is called Peter, and Andrew his brother; James the son of Zebedee, and John his brother; Philip, and Bartholomew; Thomas, and Matthew the publican; James the son of Alphaeus, and Lebbaeus, whose surname was Thaddaeus; Simon the Canaanite, and Judas Iscariot, who also betrayed him. These twelve Jesus sent forth, and commanded them, saying, Go not into the way of the Gentiles, and into any city of the Samaritans enter ye not: But go rather to the lost sheep of the house of Israel. And as ye go, preach, saying, The kingdom of heaven is at hand. Heal the sick, cleanse the lepers, raise the dead, cast out devils: freely ye have received, freely give.*

> *Luke 6:10-12* *And it came to pass in those days, that he went out into a mountain to pray, and continued all night in prayer to God. And when it was day, he called unto him his disciples: and of them he chose twelve, whom also he named apostles; Simon, (whom he also named Peter,) and Andrew his brother, James and John, Philip and Bartholomew, Matthew and Thomas, James the son of Alphaeus, and Simon called Zelotes, And Judas the brother of James, and Judas Iscariot, which also was the traitor.*

Ordination sets you apart as a forerunner of the gospel of Jesus Christ. It distinguishes you, defines your anointing and calling. Jesus appointed 12 apostles even though he had an abundance of disciples.

Ordination reveals your rank and authority over principalities and powers and your supernatural abilities.

Ordination helps establish and solidify the specific work, vision, and focus regarding the calling and mantle that is upon your life.

The apostles did not realize they were ready to be leaders. They were still striving to walk in the shadow of Jesus. But Jesus was trying to get them to make their own shadow. They were still trying to be disciples and operate through familiarity and fascination of being with Jesus and seeing the power of God at work. Jesus set them apart, so they knew they had all power and authority to perform greater works him, and this was not about elation but saving, delivering, and healing souls.

> ***Luke 10:17:20*** *And the seventy returned again with joy, saying, Lord, even the devils are subject unto us through thy name. And he said unto them, I beheld Satan as lightning fall from heaven. Behold, I give unto you power to tread on serpents and scorpions, and overall the power of the enemy: and nothing shall by any means hurt you. Notwithstanding in this rejoice not, that the spirits are subject unto you; but rather rejoice, because your names are written in heaven.*

Ordination will expose your motives and level of submissiveness for following Jesus. The apostles did not know they were truly submitted to Jesus until being faced with front line warfare of declaring whether Jesus was the Messiah and that they knew and walked with him. Because they still operated as disciples rather than ordained officers, they denied, betrayed, and abandoned Jesus, while others hid from the persecution of Jesus. They had hands on training, commissioning, and personal confirming from Jesus that they were apostles, but did not realize it was time to walk in it. After Jesus resurrected, they realized their lives were no longer business as usual.

If the apostles could have walked in Jesus shadow forever, they would have. But Jesus said in ***Matthew 9:36***, *"Then saith he unto his disciples, The harvest truly is plenteous, but the labourers are few."* Jesus did not need a fan club. He needed laborers for the gospel. He needed some ambassadors, some trailblazers, some miracle workers, some KINGDOM SHIFTERS!

Some people receive all type of training, attend limitless conferences, is at every church event, have a consistent study and prayer life, are fervent in the things of the Lord, but they hide behind their leaders or behind religious church duties and experiences. They idolize the presence and work of the Lord, yet do not realize that this dangerous or that it grieves Jesus. Licensing and ordination SHIFTS them out of hiding. It SHIFTS them from having no accountability and responsibility for what they are learning. It SHIFTS them into the forefront where they can take this great gospel to lost and dying souls.

When God revealed to me that I was an apostle and I was resistant to embracing the title, he begin to show me how some of my warfare was the enemy taking advantage of the fact that I had not become a sign of my ultimate identity in the earth; and that I had not been set in that position. He told me that I needed to position myself to be ordained. See the enemy will take your position, your land, your realms, your regions, your authority, your rewards, your blessings, and whatever else you reject or refuse to claim. He knows you own it so this is his way of recapturing it. He knows your love for God but sees your fears and insecurities. He uses that to combat you for what could be yours if you just claim it.

Fivefold ministry is not traditional church. It is equipping school. It is for the perfecting of the saints. That means you are trained and educated in the matters of God. You then graduate and go forth in demonstrating what you learned, while having seasons of obtaining more knowledge and maturity, and being released again as a laborer of Jesus.

> ***Ephesians 4:11-13*** *And he gave some, apostles; and some, prophets; and some, evangelists; and some, pastors and teachers; For the perfecting of the saints, for the work of the ministry, for the edifying of the body of Christ: Till we all come in the unity of the faith, and of the knowledge of the Son of God, unto a perfect man, unto the measure of the stature of the fulness of Christ.*
>
> ***Ephesians 1:17-18*** *that the God of our Lord Jesus Christ, the Father of glory, may give to you a spirit of wisdom and of revelation in the knowledge of Him. I pray that the eyes of your heart may be enlightened, so that you will know what is the hope of His calling, what are the riches of the glory of His inheritance in the saints.*
>
> ***Colossians 1:9-10*** *For this reason also, since the day we heard of it, we have not ceased to pray for you and to ask that you may be filled with the*

*knowledge of His will in all spiritual wisdom and understanding, so that you will walk in a manner worthy of the Lord, to please Him in all respects, bearing fruit in every good work and increasing in the knowledge of God.*

**1Peter 2:2** *Like newborn babies you should crave (thirst for, earnestly desire) the pure (unadulterated) spiritual milk, that by it you may be nurtured and grow unto [completed] salvation.*

**2Peter 3:17-18** *You therefore, beloved, knowing this beforehand, be on your guard so that you are not carried away by the error of unprincipled men and fall from your own steadfastness, but grow in the grace and knowledge of our Lord and Savior Jesus Christ To Him be the glory, both now and to the day of eternity. Amen.*

### Wisdom Keys For Aligning With Licensing And Ordination

- Unless God requires, do not submit to a ministry that does not have an established vision plan to train, mentor, license, ordain, and release saints in their calling. The Holy Spirit is going to put you in school whether man does or not. You have a choice and a right to be aligned with what Jesus is doing in your life.
- If you are a part of a ministry and they keep promising to train, mentor, license, and ordained but never follow through, seek God on whether you can attend or transition to a ministry that has these qualities. If the ministry and its leaders are to busy to make provision for them, they are stuck in works and not in kingdom business. At your job, there are required trainings you must have to fulfill policy. Some trainings align you with promotions and look good on your resume for other positions. The church has to SHIFT in fulfilling the word of the Lord regarding equipping and releasing saints. If it is not a part of the vision, then religion, laziness, or poor vision at work. God is not requiring you to submit to any of these without purpose.
- If you keep having to prove you are ready before a leader will start to train and give you opportunities to learn and labor in your God-ordained field in the gospel, then search with God as to whether you are aligned properly. Training, equipping, and opportunities are the mandate of fivefold ministry and are ongoing; it is not about proving anything. It is about being equipped, so the proof of education and training is evident in you.
- If you are at a ministry that trains, license, or ordains, but does not provide or create platform for you to be utilized, or assist you in identifying your well of release so you can join the labors of God, then explore if you should be there. Who obtains a doctorate and do not utilize it? That's right, "NO ONE!" You

will die and suffocate sitting on the pew full of knowledge and equipping that is dormant. Every minute you yield to this is every minute your destiny is dying. A lot of times leaders will say it is your character or this or that. But they are your leader. They should be helping to receive deliverance and healing so you can progress in God. I am not talking to saints who are out of order. I am talking to those who genuinely are going through the proper channels, yet dying on the pews.

- Please know that if you have a fivefold mandate, God will release vision for work. If you are at a ministry that has no vision beyond the four walls of the church and operating in the mundane "RUN!" We'll ask God if you can "RUN!" Especially if they do not release you to empower a team to fulfill that work, or release you to go and complete that assignment. Again I am not speaking to those with character issues and the like. I am talking to those who are ready in spirit and character to labor for the Lord.

A SHIFT occurs when you are being licensed or ordained. The apostles SHIFTED into a season of warfare due to SHIFTING in their calling and did not even know it. Jesus said the following to Peter.

> *Luke 22:31-34 The Amplified Bible Simon, Simon (Peter), listen! Satanhas asked excessively that [all of] you be given up to him [out of the power and keeping of God], that he might sift [all of] you like grain, But I have prayed especially for you [Peter], that your [own] faith may not fail; and when you yourself have turned again, strengthen and establish your brethren. And [Simon Peter] said to Him, Lord, I am ready to go with You both to prison and to death. But Jesus said, I tell you, Peter, before a [single] cock shall crow this day, you will three times [utterly] deny that you know Me.*

Peter thought he was ready for this SHIFT, but it was Jesus who was interceding for him. It is important to have a support system interceding for you when being in a season of licensing, ordination, or elevation. The devil will come for your truth, identity, faith, and stability. He wants you to think you are not prepared for the SHIFT. You are ready for the work and call, you just were not expecting that warfare. Peter had his guard down, but Jesus was discerning. Peter will still operate like a passionate disciple instead of a zealous apostle. Those interceding for you will help you navigate through this SHIFT successfully. Peter made a mistake, but he did not abort his calling because he had protection and covering. He was able to repent, SHIFT, and move forward in his destiny and calling.

It is my prayer that this manual will provide you with that support as it serves as a paradigm for establishing true fivefold ministries in the earth. Decreeing educational systems are implemented within our ministries to train, equip, license, ordain, and SHIFT people into living a daily life destiny soul saving. **SHIFT!**

*Homework Explorations:*
1. Journal your thoughts regarding what you learned from this chapter.
2. What negative/unhealthy comments and reactions have you heard and seen among the body of Christ regarding being licensed and ordained?
3. What are your personal thoughts about being licensed and ordained?
4. If you were to set up a fivefold ministry equipping school, what would it entail? Be specific as to its purpose, mandate, classes, opportunities, etc.

# BOOK REFERENCES

- *Apostolic Mantle By Taquetta Baker*

- *Blueletterbible.com*

- *Biblestudytools.com*

- *Dictionary.com*

- *Kingdom Decrees For Sustaining The Vision By Taquetta Baker*

- *Olivetree.com*

- *Pastoral Statistics Provided by The Fuller Institute, George Barna, Lifeway, Schaeffer Institute of Leadership Development, and Pastoral Care Inc. (https://www.pastoralcareinc.com/statistics/)*

- *Strongs Exhaustive Bible Concordance Online Bible Study Tools*

- *Sustaining The Vision Workbook by Taquetta Baker*

- *The US Army News & Information website (https://www.army.mil)*

- *Wikipedia*

- *Cover photo by Reenita Keys. Connect with her via Facebook.*

- *Editing by Amanda Latrice & Nina Cook Connect with them via Facebook.*

www.ingramcontent.com/pod-product-compliance
Lightning Source LLC
Chambersburg PA
CBHW080405170426
43193CB00016B/2820